Great Friends

DAVID GARNETT
photograph by Thomas C. Moser, Jr.

Great Friends

Portraits of seventeen writers

DAVID GARNETT

Yet meet we shall, and part, and meet again,
Where dead men meet, on lips of living men.
Samuel Butler

ISBN 0 333 25613 1

First published 1979 by
MACMILLAN LONDON LIMITED
4 Little Essex Street London WC2R 3LF
and Basingstoke
Associated Companies in Delhi, Dublin
Hong Kong, Lagos, Melbourne,
New York, Singapore and Tokyo

Printed in Great Britain at
WILLIAM CLOWES AND SONS LTD
Beccles and London

TO
Oliver William Grierson Garnett

Contents

List of Illustrations

Introduction

What follows is a conglomerate: memories as solid as cobblestones, some fragmented and perhaps distorted, all embedded in the clay of my own personality and prejudices.

Many of these sketches are early memories, but though much knowledge is hidden from the child, his eyes are sharper.

I was fortunate in my parentage. My father, Edward Garnett, was a publisher's reader from the age of eighteen until his death at sixty-nine; my mother, Constance Garnett, translated most of the nineteenth-century Russian novelists. My father's work brought him into contact with a large number of authors whom he helped to get published and advised about their work. Many friendships resulted. It is not filial piety on my part, but the fact when I say that he had a great influence on the creative literature of his time. Such a great novel as D. H. Lawrence's *Sons and Lovers* would not have been published in its present form without his help, and might not have been published until several years after it was.

My mother, Constance, exerted an indirect influence on English writers by her translations of Turgenev, Tolstoy, Dostoevsky, Gogol and Tchehov—a lifetime's work of seventy volumes from the Russian.

Throughout this book I shall refer to my parents as Edward and Constance, and the little house they had built on the boundary of Kent and Surrey below the Chart woods as The Cearne. It lies between Limpsfield and Edenbridge.

I shall write here of Edward's friends whom I knew personally and not of those with whom I had little or no contact, such as C. M. Doughty, Norman Douglas and Henry Green.

Being an only child I had no brother or sister to occupy my attention and so got into the habit of listening to the conversation of the grown-ups. I was a 'chield amang them taking notes', but as the notes were not written down at the time, there are bound to be errors.

INTRODUCTION

Besides these early memories, I shall include those writers whom I got to know later on my own account: George Moore, Virginia Woolf, Lytton Strachey and T. H. White.

Although his early works are reprinted under the name he took in later life, I have called Ford Madox Ford by the name he bore during the period when I knew him—that of Hueffer. Conversely I have called T. E. Lawrence by the name he had taken by the time I met him—that of Shaw.

I have included some passages already published elsewhere.* This is not due to laziness, but because I do not think I could improve on my original wording.

*Details of earlier publication will be found with the Acknowledgements on page 236.

A Confession of Faith

Until our times the intellectual and aesthetic requirements of ordinary people were satisfied by the vicar's sermon on Sunday. That failed to be enough. The authority and the intelligence of the clergy rapidly declined after Darwin. Attendance at church fell off as listening to stupid or intellectually dishonest clergymen became a bore.

To fill the gap, journalists, especially those who wrote in serious papers like the *Spectator, Speaker, Outlook, Nation* and *New Statesman,* mounted into the pulpit and held forth as they still do. And authors who from Defoe onwards had disguised appetising stories with religious camouflage, like so many hot-cross buns, or had sugar-coated their moralising with the enticements of sin like stale sponge cakes, became more and more popular. There have also been the straight propagandists, like Samuel Butler and George Orwell, following magnificently in the tradition of Swift.

But there have been always a few rare individuals, artists who are not concerned with preaching, or seeking a revenge upon the littleness of life, but who have accepted it, have held it up in their stories. Such writers are regarded as immoralists and as escapists by the propagandists and preachers. But in my opinion these pure artists are our best guides. The most important lesson is to understand life, not to make *a priori* judgements about it. For without complete understanding we are doomed—as mankind has been hitherto, to wars of religion, to the idealism which breeds conflicting ideologies and to final disaster. Only the artists will help us to understand life, to accept it and enjoy it.

Joseph Conrad

Joseph Conrad

He was a short and dark man, with a pointed beard, long, slightly reptilian eyes, and wearing a dark blue reefer coat. He had the manner of one whose commands are instantly obeyed, and with strangers he was exceptionally polite. With my father, Edward, he was always warm and at ease, showing the affection of a man who knows he can talk freely and always be understood. The excessive politeness, of which Ford Madox Hueffer and his biographer Professor Mizener complain, was, I guess, due to suppressed irritation. The only time I noticed it was when he was greeting unwelcome guests who were imposing themselves upon him.

My father got to know him after recommending his first book, *Almayer's Folly*, for publication, and became a close friend for life. According to Conrad it was Edward who persuaded him to give up trying to get another command and to write another book. Constance had already written on his behalf to Charles Booth, to ask whether there was a ship for him on the Booth Line. Luckily there was not.

My first memory of Conrad was when he was staying with us in the house my parents had just built, The Cearne. I was five years old.

Edward and Constance were occupied that morning, and Conrad and I went off together. There was a strong wind blowing, and it was washing-day. Mrs Collins was taking in the laundry for ironing.

Conrad must have said, 'Leave that sheet'; and the next thing I knew was that the long wickerwork washing-basket was our boat, that the sheet had been transformed into a sail, and that part of the clothes-line, attached to one corner, was in my hand and that Captain Joseph Conrad, perched on one side of the edge of the washing-basket, was giving me orders to haul in the sail or let it out. Meanwhile the grass-green waves tumbled about our cockleshell. I believe we managed to tack. Perhaps Conrad pushed our boat a few yards, so as to catch the wind on the other side. The wind blew great guns, and the sail billowed,

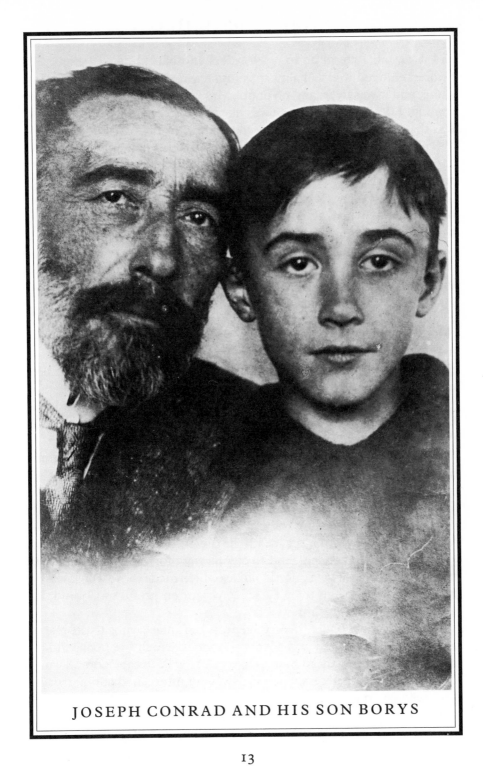

JOSEPH CONRAD AND HIS SON BORYS

and it was all I could do to obey orders and haul it flat. I believe that Conrad enjoyed that sail almost as much as I did. Then Edward came along, and it was over, and no doubt Mrs Collins carried off our sail for ironing. I don't know what he was like with other children, but Conrad was the perfect companion, or commander, for me.

Sailors cannot spend money at sea, so they splash it about when they are on land. Conrad was an example, and for many years he was in debt and constantly having to borrow more. His books did not earn enough to cover his expenses. He had great difficulty in writing, and there were black periods when he could not write at all. When such blockages occur there is nothing to be done but wait. And he could not afford to wait.

Edward had rejected a story called *Seraphina* by Ford Hueffer because it was so badly written as to be unpublishable. Yet the plot was good, and it might make an exciting story of the Robert Louis Stevenson kind. It occurred to him that Ford and Conrad might collaborate in rewriting *Seraphina*, and he hoped that Conrad would find the work easier, because it would be an adventure story and not a major work of art like *Lord Jim*, the germs of which may have been already brewing in Conrad's head.

The collaboration went on for several years. *Seraphina* transformed into *Romance* took a long time, and unfortunately did not sell. *The Inheritors*, a novel chiefly by Ford, with an incongruous touch of H. G. Wells, turned out badly. The collaboration did not solve Conrad's money troubles, and the personal relations of the two men and their wives were difficult. Conrad suffered from gout and was irritable. Ford's patronising manner, combined with his slavish admiration for Conrad, would have exasperated a saint. While Conrad was alive Ford worshipped him; after his death he invented a false image which satisfied his megalomania, and to compensate for the subordinate part he had played. As always, Ford told lies which made those who knew the truth gasp and stretch their eyes. He was often useful to Conrad, but at other times he was 'impossible'.

Fortunately a pioneer literary agent, J. B. Pinker, came to the rescue. He believed in Conrad and advanced money which the books did not earn—and then advanced more. He was losing faith that Conrad would ever be a popular success when Galsworthy intervened and persuaded Pinker to go on with his support. Success was just round the corner. It came with *Chance*. Not only did *Chance* sell, but it set the public reading the earlier books, and Conrad was established as a great writer.

EDWARD GARNETT
painting by E. M. Heath

When I was seven years old I had been reading Marryat and Ballantyne, and their stories gave rise to a question which led to my embarrassment.

Conrad was perched up on the window-sill of the 'big room' of our cottage talking to Edward, when I interrupted to ask: 'Why is the first mate of a ship always a villain?'

Conrad may have been amused, but he merely replied: 'I was a first mate myself for many years.'

15

This was not an answer. He had not denied that first mates were villains. It was possible that he had been one in his time, until he had been promoted to be the captain of a ship.

There was one visit which turned out badly. He was bringing his wife, Jessie, and his young son, Borys. I don't think his second son John had been born. At The Cearne we had only one spare room into which the whole family could not be fitted. So lodgings were taken for them in the Mill House, beside the old windmill on Limpsfield Chart. It was about a mile from our house along a track through the woods. Conrad had taught my father to drink red wine as a cure for sleeplessness, and Edward and he liked sitting up over their bottle after Constance and I had retired to bed. It was natural therefore that, rather than let Conrad stumble for a mile through the dark wood, Edward should persuade him to sleep in the spare room. Jessie Conrad was a woman prone to take offence. She felt herself neglected, put to stay in lodgings, and she made a scene with Constance. There was nothing my mother hated more than a scene. So I believe that Jessie never came to our house again.

She was capable of going to great lengths to obtain admiration. She told Elsie Hueffer that the Pent farmhouse had been besieged for two days by a mad labourer called Hunt who wanted to get hold of the maidservant. Conrad was finishing a story at the time, and Jessie knew that it would be fatal to disturb him. She therefore told him nothing about the madman, and he continued working, unaware that the butcher, baker and postman did not dare to come to the house. The story made a great impression on Constance, who declared, 'Whatever one may think of Jessie, she is a woman of great courage, and, in spite of what one might think, just the wife for Conrad.' Anyone who reads Jessie's *Joseph Conrad and his Circle* will find a completely different version there. Both were invented by her, and like so many others redound to her credit and to the discredit of her husband.

The odd thing is that there was a half-witted labourer called Hunt, for Ford and his wife, Elsie, had known him when they lived there.

Conrad, whose Polish parents had died in exile in Siberia, had good reason to hate the Russians and everything Russian. There was one exception: he had the highest admiration for Turgenev, whom he placed among the greatest masters of imaginative writing. Constance had translated all Turgenev's works, and had thereby acquired merit. But she went on to translate other Russian writers including

CONSTANCE GARNETT
painting by her sister Emmie Black

Dostoevsky, who stood for all that Conrad most disliked. Worst of all, she had many Russian friends, most of them being what Turgenev had called Nihilists—for whom Conrad felt hatred and contempt. His relationship with Constance was therefore a little like that of a well-behaved, well-bred dog in the presence of the household cat.

Perhaps if Borys and I had taken a great liking to each other things might have been different. But we did not.

It was therefore better on all counts that Jessie and Constance should not meet, and that Joseph and Edward should see each other in London, though Edward paid many visits to Conrad's house in the country, where there was no fear of Joseph meeting a Russian.

Somewhere or other I read that Conrad had drawn the wife of Little Fyne, in *Chance*, from Constance. There is, however, no resemblance. Constance never surrounded herself with young women or guided their lives. Above all things she hated giving advice. I think that the original may have been another Mrs Garnett—my uncle Robert Garnett's wife, Mattie, whom Conrad would have met through Ford and Elsie Hueffer.

My chief memory after that is of Christmas presents: a pocket compass still in my possession. It has lost its back, but the needle points to the magnetic north.

And then, when I was ten years old, I received three volumes inscribed, one by Conrad, one by Jessie, and one, I feel sure, by Conrad holding Borys's hand to guide the pen as he wrote. And with them this letter:

> Pent Farm, Stanford, near Hythe, Kent.
> 22 Dec [1902]

My dear boy,

We've sent off three volumes of the 'Leather-Stocking Tales'—one from each of us—with our love to you.

You have promised to read these stories and I would recommend you to begin with *The Last of the Mohicans*—then go on with *The Deerslayer* and end with *The Prairie*. I read them at your age in that order; and I trust that you, of a much later generation, shall find in these pages some at least of the charm which delighted me then and has not evaporated even to this day.

Thirty four years ago is a long long time to look back upon. And then already these stories were not of the day before; now the arrangement of their words has grown old—they say—very old.

It may be. Time spares no one. Even you shall grow old some day. But I have a great confidence in you; and I believe that you shall respond—as I did in my time—to the genuine feeling of the descriptions and the heroic temper of the narrative.

Your affectionate friend

> Joseph Conrad

When I was a schoolboy I may have met and greeted Conrad once or twice at Edward's Tuesday lunches at the Mont Blanc which he attended when he was in London, and to which I was sometimes taken. But I do not remember him particularly among the writers who came.

JOSEPH CONRAD

Then when I was sixteen there was a Christmas present, which I have preserved among my chief treasures. It was an American illustrated edition of *The Duel*, retitled *The Point of Honour*, originally included among *A Set of Six* and republished by itself by McClure in 1908. With the inscribed copy, was this letter:

Someries Luton
22 Dec 1908

My dear David,

Your father (who is an older friend of mine than yourself but only by some ten months or so) tells me you have read already this story. But still I send you the little volume as I want you to have something of mine, from myself, in memory of the days when we were both considerably younger—and less wise.

As the years go on you will remember those days better. For me they have a special value on which I will not enlarge at present. You were a child then, and I but an infant—a literary infant—whose first steps were—like your own—watched over by your mother and father, though I don't mean to say with the same anxious interest. That's a bond between us, surely. I think that in those days under the roof of the Cearne we were very good friends—you and I.

It pleases me to think that on some far distant day, when you are as grizzled as I am now, you may in a pause of more serious occupations, take down this little book from the shelf and glancing through it give a kind smile to my memory.

May the coming years bring you success in everything you undertake.

Your sincere friend

J. Conrad

For the last two years of the First World War, I was a conscientious objector and an agricultural labourer. I had little doubt that Conrad felt that I had failed in 'a point of honour' like Lord Jim. He probably put it down partly to my mother's involvement with Tolstoy's ideas and to Edward's pacifism. But their beliefs could not excuse my failure to do my duty. Soon after the war was over, I was staying with my friends Nicholas and Barbara Bagenal in their cottage in Kent, near Bishopsbourne where the Conrads lived. Nicholas admired Conrad's books and was anxious to meet the famous author. So he and Barbara urged me to take them to pay a call. After two years of being looked upon as a coward and a shirker, I was naturally sensitive and reluctant to expose myself.

However my hesitation was overruled, and the three of us were ushered into the drawing-room at Oswalds, where Jessie was lying on a sofa because of her bad knee, and a lady so fair as to be almost colourless greeted us. Tea and sticky conversation followed.

Suddenly Conrad came in. I could see at once that he was irritated by our intrusion. However, he greeted me kindly and asked several questions about Edward's health. Then he turned to Nicholas Bagenal. I thanked God that Nick was a Captain in the Irish Guards who had been badly wounded. Conrad became interested and talked for a little while to him, asking about his war experiences. I felt, perhaps wrongly, that Nick was an umbrella under whom I could shelter. But I hurried on our departure.

However, when I soon afterwards became a secondhand bookseller, I put Conrad on the mailing list for our catalogues. He always bought a book, usually with a friendly greeting on his postcard. The books were usually French. The only one I remember was the *Mémoires du Baron Marbot*. Conrad was always interested in everything to do with Napoleon.

Edward sent Conrad a copy of my first book and received the following letter in reply:

Oswalds, Bishopsbourne, Kent
27. 10. 22

Dearest Edward,

Many thanks for D's little tale. It is the most successful thing of the kind I have ever seen. There is somehow a slight flavour of 18th Century manner of diction which is quite fascinating. The earnest flow of the narrative has not a single uncertain note. And considering how many occasions there were to go wrong, I am impressed by the wonderful genuineness of his imagination or his surprising mastery over it. The whole psychology—man and beast—is, I should say, flawless in essence and exposition. Altogether an accomplished piece of work, touchingly amusing and without a single mistake (that I can see) in style, tone or conception. My most friendly congratulations to David on this little piece, so thoroughly done. Nothing of the amateur there. Every page holds.

So sorry dearest you had such a bad time with your veins. Mine have never played me such a trick—yet. Would you care, old friend, to see the first night of *The Secret Agent* next Thursday? I won't be there, but I'll sent you a stall? But I won't do it unless you send me word. I can't conceive anybody *wanting* to go to a theatre. Jessie's dear love.

Ever yours

J. Conrad

JOSEPH CONRAD

A few months before Conrad's death in 1924 Edward went down to stay for the weekend. As he was leaving, and the car was waiting to take him to the station, Conrad exclaimed, 'Oh, there is something I want to give you,' and rushed back into the house, to come back a minute or two later with the translation of his first book, *Almayer's Folly*, into Polish. No doubt Conrad had been gratified by being recognised in Poland. Edward could not read a word of it, but the inscription on the flyleaf made up for that.

> To Edward Garnett
> The first reader of *Almayer's Folly* in the year 1894 and ever since the dear friend of all my writing life, never failing in encouragement—and inspiring criticism
> > with love
> > Joseph Conrad.

Such warm, impulsive affection was characteristic of him.

Conrad is one of the great masters of the English language, perhaps because he came to it comparatively late in life. He makes occasional mistakes. Thus he never mastered *will* and *shall*, and wrote *irresponsive* where *unresponsive* was intended. But he doesn't fall into clichés. If he was not always a master of *le mot juste*, he was the master of *les images justes*. For example: she was not *shivering violently* where the adverb does not add to the image. No, Conrad wrote: *shivering like a dog that has been washed in hot water*.

Edward and Conrad were having a drink together, perhaps in Oddenino's. At the next table was a heavily-painted prostitute who kept looking at them. 'Look at the dirt in her nostril!' said Conrad. Edward had not noticed it. If Conrad had wished to describe the woman in a book he would have begun with that.

Conrad has been criticised for taking the 'point of honour' so frequently as his subject matter. I don't think it is the right term. His interest is more like that of the engineer studying fatigue in metals, or the effects of corrosion—the point at which the interior molecular structure can stand no more: the wire breaks, the girder snaps.

There is a breaking-point for the human spirit, when further endurance becomes impossible and the man under torture testifies to whatever is required of him. Conrad, in the person of Marlow, is actually a torturer: in the opening chapters of *Lord Jim*, Marlow tortures Jim to satisfy his curiosity. Jim has imagination: that is his dangerous weakness. Captain MacWhirr, on the other hand, who is too stupid to realise the desperate situation of his ship, the *Nan Shan*, commands Conrad's amazed respect and not the contempt he deserves as a seaman. For Conrad could never agree to Thersites' judgement of Ajax; 'I had rather be a tick in a sheep than such a valiant ignorance.' Conrad had intense powers of imagination, and in his experience at sea men like MacWhirr, with the dogged courage that is born of wooden-headed stupidity, must have provoked his envy, and he did not despise them.

He was a man of action, as well as an intellectual with the genius of imagination.

W. H. Hudson

W. H. Hudson

W. H. Hudson (I never heard him referred to by his christian names of William Henry) was a great naturalist and a still greater writer of the English language.

He was born on 4 August 1841 in a miserable little farmhouse, roofed with wooden shingles, which stood beside a row of twenty-five huge ombú trees, so that its inhabitants and their animals could enjoy the shade of the polished evergreen leaves. The nearest village was Quilmes, and it was ten miles from the capital of the Argentine republic. Buenos Aires was then a small town, and the vast plains of the pampas, covered with grazing flocks of sheep and cattle, with mile upon mile of tall grass and thistles, stretched away interminably.

Hudson's grandfather was a Devonshire man from Clyst Hydon, near Exeter, who emigrated to the United States. His son, Daniel Hudson, was born in New England and, developing tuberculosis, emigrated with his wife to the Argentine. There he became a sheep-farmer, and this English-speaking family, exiled among the wild Spanish-speaking gaucho herdsmen, lived in great poverty. W. H. Hudson was an Argentine, but he never thought of himself as one, or as a New Englander.

Two events in Hudson's boyhood determined his future. When he was fifteen he had rheumatic fever very badly, and was told that an active career was closed to him, as his heart was permanently affected. At this decisive moment an elder brother gave him Darwin's *Origin of Species*. This, and White's *History of Selborne* fired him with the ambition of becoming a great naturalist. His letters show that, when he was twenty-five, Hudson sought to become a paid collector of birds' skins for the Smithsonian Institution of Washington. His first letter, preserved in its files, contains ten simple mistakes in spelling, which reveal his unfamiliarity with the pen. The skins preserved and sent by him can be readily identified. With a later letter he sent his photograph,

W. H. HUDSON AT THE AGE OF 27

which shows him to have been an extremely handsome young man, with dark curly hair, lively eyes, a short dark beard, and an expression of eager and friendly amusement. The querulous embittered expression often to be seen in his later years is completely absent. This early photograph makes it easy to understand why the women in *The Purple Land* felt towards him as they did.

In his early manhood Hudson made several long tours, exploring different parts of the southern half of South America for himself, but never going north into the tropics. The fruits of these wandering are *The Purple Land, The Naturalist in La Plata,* and *Idle Days in Patagonia*. He was also, at this time, gathering the knowledge for his contributions to the Argentine ornithology, in which he collaborated with Sclater.

When Hudson was twenty-eight his father died, and a year later, in 1869, he obtained a passage to England.

During his first years in England most of his time was spent in London, and he had the greatest difficulty in earning a living. He was at one time secretary to a bankrupt archaeologist, who employed him in gathering materials for the concoction of pedigrees for Americans. In 1876 Hudson married Emily Wingrave, who kept a boarding-house at 11 Leinster Square, in which he was living. Mrs Hudson was several years older than he was. I have read that Hudson concealed his grey life with his wife in London, obliterating all traces of it and not allowing even his nearest friends to know of it—the implication being that he was ashamed of his wife and the dismal house in which they lived. This is entirely untrue. There is no mystery about their life. Hudson tells about it in his book *Afoot in England,* and Morley Roberts has described it in detail. For many years after their marriage the Hudsons were extremely poor. They were unable to escape from the great unfriendly wilderness of London because the boarding-house with its lodgers was their only source of livelihood. Then the boarding-house failed, and they were reduced to utter penury, though there was some improvement when Mrs Hudson inherited 40 St Luke's Road. Hudson in such surroundings was like a rare and noble creature in a cage. Those years marked him, I believe, as the beasts in the zoo are sometimes marked where they have rubbed without avail for years against the bars.

My father and Joseph Conrad, who both loved Hudson, so hated to think of this period of Hudson's life that they disliked Morley Roberts's book on Hudson which deals with it. In his prison of poverty, Hudson took refuge in books, wrote himself, got occasional articles taken in

W. H. HUDSON AS AN OLD MAN
drawing by A. D. McCormick

magazines, and slowly made a few congenial friends. It was sixteen years after his arrival in England before his first book was published. It was *The Purple Land that England Lost*, and it was only a part of a much longer romance dealing with the adventures of the hero, which Hudson destroyed. The book was a complete failure. Two years later, in 1887, *A Crystal Age* was published. It is a romance of the future and one of the strangest and most characteristic of Hudson's books. In 1892 he published a novel, *Fan*, under a pseudonym, and *The Naturalist in La Plata*, which brought him his first slight taste of success. Seventeen hundred and fifty copies sold in three years, and a third edition was printed. By this time Hudson had become a moderately prolific writer, and nine of his books were published in the ten years which followed, besides a number of pamphlets for the Society for the Protection of Birds.

GREAT FRIENDS

With the little windfalls which his books brought him, Mrs Hudson and he were able to take holidays, usually in the form of walking tours in the country, at Easter, Whitsuntide, and in the autumn. They went also on bicycling tours. Hudson's bicycle was a very solidly constructed machine, with a big frame and double bars, which he gave to my father after he had given up riding it. After 1900 Hudson's books became better known, and he was able to escape from London more often, and went for long solitary excursions to the parts of England which he liked best: Wiltshire, Hampshire, and Cornwall, the Sussex Downs, Wells in Somerset, and Wells-next-the-Sea in Norfolk. Hudson was sixty when he first met my father. Soon afterwards he came to stay with us several times.

He was tall, six foot three in height, but seemed less, as he usually stooped to listen to whomever he was talking to. He had grizzled dark hair with a curiously flat top to his head. His nose was twisted, it had been broken at some time, and he had deep-set eyes, brown with a touch of autumnal red in them, and a grizzled well-trimmed beard. To anyone today his dress would seem extraordinary, and even to my nine-year-old eyes it looked strange. His coat, made of a rough tweed, had tails with pockets in them and a waistcoat and trousers to match. He always wore a shirt with a stand-up starched white collar and starched linen cuffs, and he wore black lace-up boots. I cannot remember what kind of hat he possessed: he was always bare-headed in my memory.

He was a quiet and a silent man whose emotions were kept hidden; only after getting to know him could one tell that there was an ember glowing within, which could be sometimes blown into flame. I was in a fortunate position to get to know him, as at that age and for years afterwards my chief interest was in natural history, and my greatest pleasure was in watching the birds and spying on the wild creatures that lived in the great wood behind our house. There were red squirrels, stoats and weasels—I once saw a pine marten—foxes, hares and, of course, multitudes of rabbits, which my dog Nietzsche hunted, and I roasted over a fire in the wood.

My solitary pursuits must have brought back memories of his own boyhood. Hudson treated me from the first as an equal, invited me to accompany him on his walks and to show him my discoveries: birds' nests, squirrels' dreys and so on. Early in our friendship I had two triumphs. I told Hudson that I had seen an unusual frog near the pond at Trevereux, and, greatly daring, for it was forbidden territory, I took him to look for it.

W. H. HUDSON

I see us then, in an odd moment of self-consciousness: Hudson, tall, respectable, treading warily over the oozy verge between the white poplar trees that surrounded the pond, I lagging behind a little, obsessed by two fears: that my strange frog should not be visible and that the Trevereux gardener or gamekeeper should come up and order us off for trespassing. Hudson had no such cares. He trod carefully so as not to sink in the mud, and stealthily so as to have every chance of seeing my frog. What was wonderful was that he had complete faith in my story. Anyone else would have brushed it on one side as a child's invention. We must have waited there for some time, and I grew increasingly anxious, for the pond lay on the edge of the Trevereux orchard, close to the house. Its waters were dark and oily, with no water weed, the bottom black with dead leaves. And Hudson stood there absolutely silent, and I watched him with a sinking heart. But the vigil was not fruitless. He pointed, and there was my frog—or rather toad, for Hudson was able to identify him. He was *Bufo calamita* the natterjack or running toad, distinguished by his short hind legs and a stripe down the back.

We always walked through the woods in silence so as to have a better chance of seeing the wild creatures. Once I remember he halted. A bird was singing. He asked me if I knew the song of the missel thrush. I said I did not. Together we drew nearer, and, though I did not see the bird, Hudson presently pointed to a nest, rather high up in the branches of a small oak tree. No doubt the mate of the singing bird was on her nest, but we went away without disturbing her. I have always had a bad ear for bird song—except for the obvious ones—and though I tried to remember the difference between that of a song thrush and a missel thrush, I soon became uncertain.

My second triumph must have been later in the summer. One evening, after my proper bedtime, my parents and Hudson strolled into the summer night, and I ran after them. There were glow-worms, and I interrrupted the conversation to tell Hudson that I had seen something phosphorescent on the ground, and after bringing a light, I saw it was a small centipede and not a glow-worm. I think my mother began to scold me for making up a tale. But Hudson said I was quite right: there was such a centipede or millipede, and my memory is that he said it was rare.

It was probably that night that we went on into the next field to listen to the nightjars churring. Then Hudson made us all hide under some gorse bushes. We sat silent, though the prickles were difficult to endure, and Hudson imitated the birds' churring, vibrating rattle and then after

29

a few minutes we were rewarded by the birds flying over our hiding place and clapping their wings together when we were discovered.

In the evening I remember my father and Hudson sitting over the log fire sipping the Spanish Valdepeñas red wine which Hudson had introduced on account of its cheapness. It was a thousand times better than the Australian Keystone Burgundy supplied by the Westerham grocer. But which of them was it who said that the valley where it grew was deep and almost inaccessible, and that the muleteers who brought it out allowed many barrels to fall upon the rocks, so that they could drink their contents, and for that reason supplies of it were scanty?

I think that it must have been Hudson who invented the story, for I went on believing it till I visited Spain and found that Valdepeñas grows on a flat plain and is the commonest of Spanish wines outside Catalonia. If my father had invented the tale, I should not have believed it implicitly or for so long.

I remember one occasion when they were sitting there, Edward telling Hudson that his real talent was in describing character, and that he wasted it writing about adders and Dartford warblers. Hudson suddenly got angry. A red light came into his eyes, and he burst out: 'I am a naturalist. I care nothing about people. I write about what I observe. I don't care for made-up stories that amuse people like you.'

Edward was secretly delighted at having enraged Hudson and would then pick out some bit from *The Purple Land* to prove his point, while Hudson glared at him angrily and then subsided, as though Edward were not worth powder and shot, and the red light would go out of his eyes.

My father was being cruel, though not consciously so. For when Hudson began to write his subjects had been people, and he had starved. And it was not until he wrote as a naturalist that he had made a slender living by his pen. He had torn up much of what he wrote, and it came as an astonishment to him that after Edward had coaxed the manuscript of *Green Mansions* out of him, it should eventually prove the most successful of all his books.

While I was still a young boy, he gave me a copy of his *British Birds*, which is a bad book because he deliberately omitted some of our rare visitors lest collectors should be put on the watch for them. Most modern ornithologists have in the same way left out descriptions of the nesting habits and illustrations of birds' eggs, in order not to help collectors.

Two other books he gave me were his own *A Little Boy Lost*, which I did not much care for, and a book of Barrie's which I disliked so much that I sent it back to him with a letter to say why I thought it so bad! Except for *The Twelve-Pound Look* and one or two short plays, J. M. Barrie's work has always seemed to me mawkish.

It was not until 1906, when my mother and I lived in a workman's flat in Hampstead, that we went off to pay a call on Mrs Hudson at 40 St Luke's Road in Bayswater.

It was one of those horrid little grey brick and slate-roofed houses built for the teeming lower middle classes in Victorian London. Mrs Hudson was a frail little old woman, with dark eyes, dressed in black. I, naturally, felt no interest in her at all, while she and Constance sat making conversation and drinking tea. But they must have liked each other, for the calls were repeated, and on one occasion Hudson was present. What impressed me then was the gentleness and affection with which he addressed her. There was a total absence of the aloof touch of bitterness he so often showed. It was clear that he loved her and wanted to make her happy.

A few years later my father used occasionally to take me to have lunch at the Mont Blanc restaurant in Gerrard Street on a Tuesday when a number of his friends—all of them writers—met together. Conrad was sometimes there; Hilaire Belloc, H. M. Tomlinson, Stephen Reynolds, Perceval Gibbon, Thomas Seccombe, Muirhead Bone and other forgotten figures of the literary world before the first war are among those who sometimes came. Fairly regular attendants were Hudson and Edward Thomas, and as both of them were my particular friends, I usually managed to sit beside one of them—once between them. It must have been through such meetings that Hudson, who had few close friends and lived in solitude after his wife's death, became very much attached to Edward Thomas. Hudson was often very much on the defensive with my father, his publisher's reader and adviser. But I believe that his heart went out to Edward Thomas without reservation. And though so different in age, they had many things in common: a great love for the country, particularly of the South and West of England, and both were gifted writers who had had to turn out books to make a bare living.

I did not see Hudson after my early adolescence until after the war, when I had become a bookseller. By then *Green Mansions* had been published in the United States—nearly fifteen years after it had appeared in England—and it had at once become a best-seller. When Hudson had been very ill in hospital Edward had taken him a copy of

Aksakov's *Years of Childhood,* and that had set Hudson thinking of his own. He at once began one of his most delightful books, *Far Away and Long Ago.*

Success had come to him in his old age, but instead of mellowing him, as is usual, it had roused and increased his bitterness. Just as when Edward had told him that *El Ombú* (a story written as part of the original of *The Purple Land*) was a masterpiece, Hudson had glared at him in rage—a rage not, I think, far from tears—so success when it came seemed a worthless mockery. He hated the men and women who worship it and are ready to crush the individuality of others to achieve it, whether to satisfy their own wants or to carry on the business of the world. Hudson had no interest in the business of the world. He hated the way it was carried on, nature being despoiled and beautiful birds and animals exterminated. In all his writings one finds a fierce discrimination—an awareness that the majority are not good or beautiful or lovable, but that here and there, scattered amongst them, there is a minority of more beautiful, tender-hearted, finer beings.

At the end of *The Purple Land* he makes the reflection:

I cannot believe that if the country had been conquered and recolonised by England, and that all that is crooked in it made straight, according to our notions, my intercourse with the people would have had the wild, delightful flavour I have found in it. And if that distinctive flavour cannot be had along with the material prosperity resulting from Anglo-Saxon energy, I must breathe the wish that this land may never know such prosperity.

He was in this bitter mood when I met him again. He wrote and said that he had a number of his books at St Luke's Road that he wished to sell, and would I call on him? There, laid out on a sofa, were a number of his books, first editions—only a few of those he wrote had had a second.

He was rather suspicious of me; perhaps he thought that I should trade on our earlier friendship and swindle him. But I think I satisfied him that I was as honest as is possible for a shopkeeper who has to make a profit, selling things for more than he pays for them.

I had, however, a confession to make which startled him. Edward had told me of the existence of Hudson's youthful novel, *Fan,* published under a pseudonym. It had been a total failure. I advertised for it for many weeks in the secondhand booksellers' trade paper, *The Clique,* and had succeeded in being offered two rather battered copies for about half-a-crown each. I told Hudson this, and he looked for a moment as though he thought I were going to blackmail him.

However, I went on to say that I knew that he did not wish his authorship known, and that I had kept it secret even from my partners, and would not sell either copy until the secret was known after his death. This reassured him, but when I went on to tell him that I had read *Fan* and that there were parts of it that I liked very much, he was—not angry as he used to be with Edward—but upset. He tried to tell me it was worthless, but the mention of the book had raised memories which were painful. I picked up my purchases and went away. He was, I suppose, satisfied with the prices I had paid him, for he wrote again not long afterwards, and said that he had more books to sell, so I went again to St Luke's Road. He was eighty-two and kept alive by digitalis, as I am now, until he died. My sorrow was mixed with an egotistic regret that he had not read my first book, which was published a week or two later. I should have liked his opinion of it more than most peoples'.

My regret now is that when we walked about the High Chart woods together, we had never come across an adder. For I love snakes as much as he did, and I believe that he would sometimes pick an adder up by its tail and hold it at arm's length, confident that it had not the strength to double up and strike the hand that held it, with its poison fangs. It would have been wonderful to have seen him do that. There was the same wild delightful flavour and beauty in the man as in the birds he watched and the snake he held so fearlessly before letting it rustle away to enjoy its own life.

Ford Madox Hueffer

Ford Madox Hueffer

I cannot write about Ford Madox Ford, whom I never met—nor about his work having only read about ten out of the eighty-one books that he published over that name. I write therefore about him when he was Hueffer, and I knew him personally and he was kind to me, and about his relations with my family. Those who want to know more of his life, in which he played many parts, should turn to Arthur Mizener's biography *The Saddest Story*, though I must warn them it contains many inaccuracies, and to the forthcoming book by my friend, Tom Moser.

Ford's heredity is important in order to understand his life and character. His father, Franz Hüffer, the youngest of seventeen children, came of a well-to-do, ardently Catholic, middle-class, German family, who owned a printing works and a newspaper. Perhaps because he became an atheist, he emigrated to England, anglicised his name to Francis Hueffer—which he pronounced Hoofer—and married the daughter of that great Pre-Raphaelite painter Ford Madox Brown, by his second wife, the sixteen-year-old daughter of a farmer, who is said to have rescued the artist from her father's bull.

Madox Brown's elder daughter, Lucy, had married William Michael Rossetti, the brother of Dante Gabriel and Christina Rossetti. Their mother was a descendant of that Dr William Polidori who was Byron's secretary and a friend of Shelley's—it was therefore very natural for Ford to grow up thinking that the only worthy life was that of a poet, writer or artist.

This was reinforced by his friendship with the Garnett family. My grandfather, Richard Garnett, a poet, scholar and author, was a close friend and neighbour of William Michael Rossetti and also of Ford Madox Brown. Francis Hueffer was a musicologist and a Wagnerian, who was the author of books on the Troubadours and Provençal poetry. He wrote librettos for operas and was the music critic of *The Times*. He

FORD MADOX HUEFFER

died when Ford was sixteen, leaving his widow almost penniless. She went with her younger son, Oliver, to live with her father two doors away from the Rossettis. Close by were their friends, the Garnetts.

After Richard Garnett became Keeper of Printed Books he had an official residence in the British Museum. Ford wrote later: 'I was in and out of the Garnett house in the Museum Courtyard every day and all day long. Their hospitality was as boundless as it was beneficent.' There he would meet Edmund Gosse, Samuel Butler, Sidney Colvin and, perhaps rather surprisingly, Oscar Wilde.

Robert Garnett, the eldest son, was seven years older than Ford, and Edward Garnett five. It was therefore natural that Ford should look up to the older Garnett boys. Both played a large part in Ford's earlier years. There was, however, a deep temperamental difference between the young Garnetts, who were sceptical, unworldly and over-critical, and the two Hueffer boys, who were credulous, worldly (without being worldly-wise) and over-confident. The Garnett boys were inclined to regard Ford and his brother Oliver as half egregious asses and half charlatans. There is little doubt they were right as regards Oliver. He is alleged to have purloined his grandfather's gold watch and chain on more than one occasion and then to have cheerfully presented the indulgent old man with the pawn ticket. He was heavily in debt for most of his life, largely because he wanted to cut a dash. He was the fattest man I have seen in army uniform—a Goering without the medals.

Ford was more complicated than Oliver, for he had talent and industry, which the Garnetts may have under-rated. But he suffered from the same love of extravagance as Oliver. Ford who originally respected the Garnetts, became more and more exasperated by their scepticism and their almost puritanical contempt for notoriety and the trappings of success, which constituted the breath of romance for Ford. But the process of disillusionment was slow, and for many years Robert and Edward went on being useful friends.

Ford's first book was a story he had made up to amuse his sister, Juliet. He showed it to his grandfather and to Edward, and they were delighted. Ford Madox Brown made two illustrations for it—I have the drawing for the frontispiece hanging on my wall as I write—and Edward persuaded his employer Fisher Unwin to include *The Brown Owl* in the series, 'The Children's Library', that he was launching.

While at his preparatory school Ford had met Elsie Martindale, and she had fallen in love with him. When he was eighteen and she fifteen, their love for each other was resumed. Elsie's father Dr William

Martindale, a successful pharmacist with a shop in New Cavendish Street, who had written *The Extra Pharmacopeia*, a standard work, and lectured on *materia medica*, disapproved of the attachment; and when Ford was twenty and Elsie seventeen, he forbade him the house and was prepared to prevent clandestine meetings by keeping Elsie locked up. Robert Garnett was then a young solicitor of twenty-seven, and he played a part which might have injured his career if the facts had come out in court. He helped Elsie, who was being made a ward of court, to run away from home and vanish—going to stay with some Garnett relatives in Bath. Later she took refuge with other friends of Robert's in Gloucester, and he advised Ford and Elsie to get married as soon as possible. When the case was heard before Mr Justice North, Ford announced: 'There is no Miss Elsie Martindale—she is Mrs Ford Madox Hueffer.' Ford was warned that he had exposed himself to criminal proceedings, but the couple were allowed to go free.

They went to live on the edge of Romney Marsh—always Ford's spiritual home. In due course a baby, Christina, was born, and a reconciliation between Elsie and her parents was patched up.

Three years later they came to live in my aunt Grace's cottage, which she had just had built half a mile from my parents' house, although she herself lived in Ceylon.

Ford was then assuming the part of a peasant and was dressed in a smock frock, corduroys, gaiters and hob-nailed boots, and carried an ashplant stick in his hand. He was, he said, 'a small producer', but the only signs were making a vegetable garden and keeping ducks. As there was no water, a hip-bath was sunk in the ground for them to splash in. They were called after my mother and my aunts, and Ford would try to tease them by such remarks as 'Lucy is such a greedy duck. She always snatches the worms from Connie,' for the ducks followed him as he dug the garden. 'We roasted Katie last Sunday, but she was terribly tough.'

At my first meeting with Ford, when I was five years old, I am reported to have asked, 'Who's that man with hay on his face?' Which is peculiar, as I had been well broken in to beards by that of Stepniak and the splendid beard of Prince Kropotkin which spread all over his chest and reached to the second button of his waistcoat. But Ford's beard did not last long.

My first actual memory of him was when he squatted down and came leaping towards me like a gigantic frog—I was equally delighted when he showed me that he could twitch his ears independently. He liked to amuse children, and was a delightful companion for the young.

He was then a tall young man with very fair hair, prominent blue eyes, pink cheeks and a rather fishy mouth, usually open, under a drooping moustache. He was very Germanic in appearance.

It is difficult for me to realise that Elsie was then only a girl of twenty, nearer to me in age than she was to my mother of thirty-six. She was tall, high-breasted and dark, with a bold eye and a rich, high colour like a ripe nectarine. She dressed in richly coloured garments in the William Morris style, prevalent among ladies of the aesthetic group, and entirely unlike the fashionable white blouse high in the neck, belt and full skirt— usually worn with a straw hat, of the 'Gibson Girl'. I was at once greatly attracted by her, and soon after meeting her I proposed marriage, and when she pointed out that Ford was an obstacle, I said cheerfully that it would be a good thing if he died soon. Ford was informed of my intention of superseding him, but he bore no rancour and continued to be a most charming entertainer of my childhood.

One day a family of Russian political exiles descended upon us, coming not from Siberia, but Paris, where David Soskice had been married long enough to have a son of my age, called Victor. An empty cottage was found for them at Kent Hatch, but Madame Soskice did not care for damp English cottages, and having decided to part from her husband, went back to Paris, taking Victor with her.

David Soskice was a squarely built man with a curly black beard, a square forehead and the simplest ideas of right and wrong, which he put into practice with little regard for consequences. For example, he believed that Captain Dreyfus was innocent, and he believed that one should tell the truth in all circumstances—a far more doubtful proposition. So finding himself in the middle of a crowd in Paris, howling for Dreyfus to be guillotined, Soskice shouted 'Vive Dreyfus'. Only the solidity of his construction saved him from being torn in pieces. He had a literal mind and no imagination. What he liked were facts, and Ford was delighted to supply them.

D. H. Lawrence, who did not meet Ford until ten years or more after the event, must have heard about it from me or my parents, and he loved to give imitations of Ford walking up and down drawling out: 'Yaws . . . yaws . . . Rye is the largest of our crops . . . but we export it all to Prussia and Poland,' while Soskice sat on the doorstep and scribbled it in his notebook. Ford also told Soskice that the most profitable crop was giant kale, for every soldier in the British army had to carry a swagger-stick under his arm, and the swagger-sticks were made from the stems of the kale. It was not, however, only Soskice's appetite for statistics that kept him so often at Grace's cottage. For it was there that he met Juliet. Ford's sister was a most lovely creature, like the princess in a fairy story. She had a wild rose complexion, masses of golden hair and enormous innocent blue eyes. And in spite of increasing *embonpoint*, she kept her beauty all her life.

David Soskice fell in love with this glorious creature, and, more surprisingly, Juliet fell in love with him. He was the antithesis of her brothers, being a man of the strictest integrity whose every word could be relied on. Soskice was able and industrious and was a qualified Russian lawyer. Juliet had a great capacity for enjoying life and a rich sense of humour, which her husband could not share. She was also more gifted than he was. Her translations of Nekrassov in two volumes of the 'World's Classics' are the best translations of Russian poetry in English. Mizener's statement that Juliet learned Russian to help Constance Garnett with her translations is nonsense. She learned it because her husband was Russian. The marriage of this strangely assorted pair was a happy one. They had two sons, the elder of whom was the late Lord Stow Hill, formerly Attorney-General.

While the Hueffers were still at Grace's cottage, my father introduced Ford to that brilliant American story-writer, Stephen Crane, who was living temporarily at Oxted with his wife, Cora.

Marjorie Pease, the public-spirited and active wife of the secretary of the Fabian Society, made great friends with Cora Crane, and they kept up correspondence after Stephen's death when Cora went back to be the madame of her brothel in Florida, to which she had charitably taken Stephen Crane after he was shipwrecked. I do not think Cora had confided her plans or her profession to her Scottish friend, who was easily scandalised by any extra-marital relations.

Edward also introduced Conrad to Ford, who describes their first meeting:

Conrad came round the corner of the house. . . He was in advance of Mr Garnett, who had gone inside, I suppose to find me. Conrad stood looking at the view. His hands were in the pockets of his reefer-coat, the thumbs sticking out. His black, torpedo beard pointed at the horizon. He placed a monocle in his eye. Then he caught sight of me.

I was very untidy in my working clothes. He started back a little. I said: 'I'm Hueffer'. He had taken me for the gardener.

His whole being melted together in enormous politeness. His spine inclined forward: he extended both hands to take mine. He said:

'My dear faller. . . Delighted. . . Ench. . .anté.'

That rings true—except that it shows that Ford had never seen a torpedo.

It was at that meeting, or soon after, that 'Mr' Garnett, as Edward became after Ford had quarrelled with him, suggested that Ford and Conrad should collaborate in rewriting *Seraphina*. As Ford claimed later that he had taught Conrad how to write English—Conrad had published *Almayer's Folly*, *The Outcast of the Islands* and, perhaps the best of his longer books, *The Nigger of the 'Narcissus'*, before he met him—it is relevant to quote his biographer Arthur Mizener: 'the style of much of Ford's work up to the time of his collaboration with Conrad has a wooden solemnity it is hard to believe Ford was ever capable of'.

When Henry James was told of the project for collaboration by Elsie and my aunt Olive, he commented: 'To me this is like a bad dream which one relates at breakfast.' After which the ladies said no more.

I think that Ford's *Seraphina*, after it had been transformed into *Romance*, is a rattling good story, but that *The Inheritors* has no merit, in spite of the very flattering portrait of Edward as Lee, the critic with infallible literary judgement.

But before either of these books was published, and when I was about seven years old, I went with my parents to Aldington Knoll to visit Ford and Elsie, after they had left Grace's cottage. The knoll itself was a steep grassy little hill, and the cottage nestled below it. Running down the left-hand side of the garden was a swiftly flowing brook, and across it Ford had installed the most fascinating waterwheel which appeared to be turned by two little wooden figures in red jackets and green breeches, standing one each side of the brook. Actually it was the rushing stream that kept their arms turning so industriously. I think I was more fascinated by it than the two- or three-year-old Christina. I have a vague memory of our going to see the Conrads at the Pent, a small farmhouse which Ford had bought before coming to live at Grace's cottage, and which he had let to Conrad.

While we were at Aldington Knoll we were driven over to Brede Place, near Rye, to see Crane and his wife, who were living in that wonderful old house on a lavish, if improvised, scale. Henry James accompanied us, riding on a bicycle. Once again I can remember the house, but not the people—by which I mean Stephen and Cora Crane. My only clear memory of Stephen Crane is seeing him and Conrad and Edward standing talking at the bottom of the Cearne garden. Of Brede Place I remember a leper's window in the wall of the Chapel so that the

HENRY JAMES WITH HIS BICYCLE
(another photograph, not the author's)

lepers from the neighbouring pesthouse could, my mother explained, listen to the service without infecting those inside.

The next time we saw the Hueffers, they had moved from Aldington Knoll to Winchelsea, and we stayed in lodgings next door to them. The

Boer War was drawing to a close. It was perhaps the late summer of 1901. But I may have remembered it as autumn because there was a flower show with a military band in green uniforms and felt hats turned up on one side, that played *The Last Rose of Summer*, through a long, hot and dusty afternoon. I had been given a Brownie Kodak box camera. A few days after our arrival, Ford took us over in a hired wagonette to Rye, and we called on Henry James at Lamb House. We found him dressed in an extremely tight-fitting pair of knickerbockers and an equally exiguous jacket of black and white checks. When he came out and showed us round Rye, he wore on his large head a cap of the same shepherd's plaid check. In this costume he was kind enough to pose for me, and the photograph I took came out perfectly, but has, alas, long since been lost. Lamb House astonished me by its tidiness, the beautiful polished furniture, the perfection of the hall and drawing-room and the beautiful garden. Ford, tall and fresh-coloured, smiling and showing his rabbit teeth, enjoyed himself patronising my parents on one side and James on the other. Perhaps Edward and Constance were aware of the possibility that they were being thrust on the Master by Ford. If they were right in that suspicion, I am duly grateful to Ford, for I should not otherwise have had tea with Henry James in Lamb House. He walked back a little way with us, and we said goodbye on the edge of Rye and walked down from the high ground to where our conveyance was waiting.

While we were at Winchelsea, Ford showed us round its ancient defences dating from before the sea had receded and left it high and dry. I think what he told us then was true, and that he really knew what he was talking about. There was less of that slow drawl in his voice which helped to give him time to make up his inventions. And of course we all made the long walk to the sea, and Edward went for a swim, while Christina and I paddled and played on the beach.

After the visit to Winchelsea I don't think I saw Elsie again. That beautiful young wife and mother was to become a tragic figure. From the age of fifteen she had taught herself to look at the world through Ford's eyes. During the years of courtship and early marriage he had been first something of an Anarchist like his Rossetti cousins. Then he became a William Morris Socialist with a nostalgia for the medieval, which expressed itself in a society of hand-weavers, smallholders, craftsmen and poets. Ford's transition from Peasant to Great Writer was not too difficult, but she became bewildered and antagonised by those which followed. For Ford adopted in rapid succession the roles of Man-

44

FORD MADOX HUEFFER

About-Town, Tory Squire, Ardent Catholic, German Baron and Patriotic British Officer.

During these transformations, Elsie stood like a land bird, her feet firmly planted on dry land on the edge of a lake in which Ford, that domestic duck, was trying desperately to keep up with such strange waterfowl as Ezra Pound and Hemingway and Joyce.

A woman like 'The Darling', in Tchehov's story of that name, could have adapted herself easily, but Elsie was not a chameleon. She clung to Ford's early beliefs and became an embittered shrew.

About four years after our stay in Winchelsea I was alone at our home in the country: Edward and Constance were in London. There was a knock at the door, and there was Ford. He had come to see Constance on some urgent business.

He was terribly upset to find he had missed them, but he stayed and had tea with me, and I walked back with him to Westerham through Squerries Park. He had been cheerful, but a mood of melancholy came over him, and he sang one melancholy song after another, some French, some German, and ending with the Westmorland folk-song *Poor Old Horse*. Ford's voice was not bad, his ear was good, and the expression he put into the words of the horse's cruel master was pathetic in the extreme.

> You are old, you are old, you are deaf, dull, dumb and slow
> You are not fit for anything, or in my team to draw.
> You have eaten all my hay, you have spoiled all my straw,
> So hang him, whip, stick him, to the huntsman let him go.

And in the most unhappy voice, Ford broke in to say something like this: 'I am that poor old horse, David. I am old, and I am cold. And I am no longer fit for anything. They do not pity me, David, but throw me aside . . .' And then he began to sing the verses over again.

> My clothing was once of the linsey-wolsey fine.
> My tail it grew at length.
> My coat did likewise shine;
> But now I'm growing old.
> My beauty do decay,
> My master frowns upon me.
> One day I heard him say:
> 'Poor old Horse, poor old Horse.'

And then Ford continued: 'The world is very cruel to the old, David. It is very cruel to me. . . Once I was a brilliant young poet, a famous writer

45

. . . now I'm no more use to anyone, and they kick me now they have got me down. . . Poor old horse. . .'

I took Ford's hand in mine and squeezed it. I was in tears; and, seeing this, Ford wept also; then brushed his tears aside for a moment to look at his watch and make sure he was not late for the train.

I said we all loved and admired him; we hurried on, and by the time we had reached Westerham, Ford had wiped his tears away and begun to tell me some cheerful story. For several years afterwards I felt a particular tenderness for him when I recollected this scene, and I defended him fiercely from Edward's cynical criticisms.

The Victorians of a generation earlier were given to self-pity. Virginia Woolf describes how her father, Leslie Stephen, used to beat his breast and complain to Vanessa, 'You stand there silent. Don't you pity me?' when she presented the weekly housekeeping bills, before he would sign a cheque.

Ford was only thirty-five at most when he gave the display in Squerries Park. He had still to write his best books. I think he was, for my benefit, dramatising the song. There would have been no tears had he been alone: he needed an audience. I think Dickens might possibly have behaved in the same way.

It was soon after that visit that we began to see more of Ford, who was planning the *English Review*. Ford was living in Holland Park Avenue, and he began to give literary parties, one of which I remember very well. It was a poetical contest of *bouts-rimés*. Of those who took part I remember Dollie Radford, who won first prize, Hilaire Belloc, who won the second, and Ezra Pound. I think that Ernest Rhys and his wife were also competitors.

But apart from that party I went to Ford's flat at other times, for I met Stephen Reynolds there with his enormous Great Dane dog—as big as a calf—which embarrassed Reynolds by walking into butchers' shops and helping herself to a sirloin, or a leg of lamb. She would trot home followed by a butcher's boy, and Reynolds would have to pay up. Stephen Reynolds was the author of a successful book *A Poor Man's House* about Bob Woolley and his brother, who were Brixham fishermen. After its publication he brought Bob Woolley to London, and they went about together wearing blue jerseys, I suppose to prove Reynolds's *bona fides*.

Ford on the other hand became very grand, wearing an overcoat with an astrakhan collar, well-pressed trousers, with spats and a top hat. He was becoming not only a literary lion but a Man-About-Town, and was on the way to becoming a Tory Country Gentleman. Edgar Jepson, whom he patronised at this time, said: 'Ford told me about his life as a country gentleman, but I never saw his horses.'

During his short reign as the editor, the *English Review* became the finest literary monthly in the history of English letters. Thomas Hardy, Tolstoy, Henry James, H.G. Wells, Arnold Bennett, John Galsworthy were among the established authors to contribute, and it contained the first important publications of D. H. Lawrence and Ezra Pound.

Ford was by nature optimistic and wildly extravagant, and it could not last. He developed *la folie de grandeur* and vanity, and his capacity for invention grew. But Ford did not always believe that what he said was true. Edward had got one of Ford's books published, and it had done very well—twelve hundred copies being subscribed. So Ford and Edward had lunch together to celebrate. A journalist came up and asked Ford how his new book was doing'

'It has just sold twelve thousand copies,' said Ford, 'and they are busy reprinting.'

When the journalist had gone, Edward asked Ford how he could tell such lies. 'My dear Edward,' replied Ford, 'truth is relative. If I had told that man that my book had sold twelve hundred copies, he wouldn't have understood. But when I told him it had sold twelve thousand copies he was astonished to precisely the same degree that you and I are astonished because it has sold twelve hundred. Truth is relative.'

Ford liked Constance and felt respect for her, so that when his troubles started, she believed that he was being torn in pieces by unscrupulous and vindictive women. Elsie's sister, Mary Martindale, used to visit our little flat in Hampstead to seek advice and confide her troubles. Constance disliked confidences, particularly about sexual matters, which she believed concerned only the persons involved.

Edward thought that Ford behaved with abominable treachery to Arthur Marwood who had put up money which enabled the *English Review* to come into existence. Naturally enough Marwood became anxious about Ford's extravagance. Ford took offence and accused Marwood of taking credit for the *Review*. Then Elsie took a hand. She had had a serious operation costing £440 (paid by Marwood), and her recovery was slow. Marwood became attracted by her and wrote her indiscreet letters. She informed Ford, who told her to send the letters to their solicitor, Robert Garnett. Love letters are only sent to solicitors when some legal action is contemplated.

Edward believed that Ford was mad enough to wish to cite

Marwood as co-respondent in a divorce suit and claim damages, or to use the letters to blackmail Marwood.

As Ford was living with a German girl he had picked up in the Empire Lounge—then the parade ground of expensive prostitutes—had been having an affair with Elsie's sister and had just embarked on one with Violet Hunt, he would have been mad indeed. Perhaps he was.

All the parties concerned confided in Conrad, who wrote to Galsworthy:

[Ford's] conduct is impossible . . . He is a megalomaniac who imagines he is managing the Universe and that everybody treats him with the blackest ingratitude. A fierce and exasperating vanity is hidden under his calm manner which misleads people. I do not hesitate to say that there are cases, not quite so bad, under medical treatment.

What was the reason for Elsie's behaviour? Wives are very apt to tell their husbands about attentions paid them by another man, particularly if the lover is cooling off and they want to squeeze all the emotional excitement possible out of the situation. She may have hoped that by exciting Ford's jealousy she could induce him to return to her and live in the country.

Edward, I feel certain, believed that Ford had planned to 'frame' Marwood. If he had evidence of this, he did not reveal it to Constance, or I believe to Conrad, who continued to see Ford occasionally and receive letters from him, though he was on Marwood's side. Edward never spoke to Ford again, and Robert, after trying to smooth down the relations between the parties, ceased to act as Ford's solicitor.

Ford had become involved with Violet Hunt, and one of her novels had been running as a serial in the *English Review*. After Ford had been dismissed from the editorship by the new proprietor, he went to live with Violet Hunt at South Lodge, Campden Hill. Violet Hunt belonged to the wealthy bourgeoisie—upper classes—who were extremely conventional about the outward appearances of sexual relations. Scandal spread about Ford and Violet, in spite of Violet's semi-imbecile mother and then of Elsie's sister, Mary Martindale, chaperoning them. Later Ford's mother joined them. Ford was hoping that Elsie would divorce him, which she was reluctant to do.

Violet was a thin viperish-looking woman, past her first beauty, with a thin pointed chin, and deep-set burning, brown eyes. There was a driving force within her—insatiable ambition. Edward seldom met her,

VIOLET HUNT

except at funerals. Before going, many years later, to that of W. H. Hudson, he opened a copy of the *Daily Mail* and read an article by Violet Hunt describing how 'old Huddie' was devoted to her, and how she had forced her way in to where his corpse was lying and had seen a spot of blood on the sheet. Edward was disgusted, but he had hardly arrived at the cemetery when Violet rushed up.

'Oh, Mr Garnett, we never seem to meet except on these sad occasions.'

Edward cut her short with: 'Perhaps one of us two will be the next. So let us make a self-denying ordinance. I will promise not to come to your funeral, if you will promise not to come to mine.'

When I was seventeen Ford heard that my mother was worrying about my education and wrote to her: 'Send David to me for a few years, Connie, and I will teach him to write like Flaubert.'

The invitation was not taken seriously, and I was denied the opportunity of sharing with Joseph Conrad the privilege of having been taught to write by Ford. Actually I wanted to be a biologist.

I had decided to enter the Imperial College of Science in South Kensington, and as Violet Hunt was acquainted with the wife of the Professor of Zoology, Adam Sedgwick, Ford suggested that if I would turn up at South Lodge at three o'clock, Violet would take me to call on Professor Sedgwick. With the unimpeachably respectable background of her own mother and Ford's mother as chaperones, Violet did not hesitate to show herself everywhere, dragging Ford round with her. From the conventional, Edwardian point of view, this was foolish. Violet had a touch of the Elizabethan pirate in her, and refusing to keep quiet, organised rounds of social visits for them both, as though bent on singeing Mrs Grundy's beard. Such behaviour invited gossip and scandal among the censorious.

And so in the early summer of 1910, Ford and Violet, with me on the seat opposite, went bowling down Church Street in an open hired carriage of the kind called a victoria. We were going round Sloane Street and South Kensington, to leave cards and pay formal calls. Ford had his top hat on his knees and Violet card-cases at hand and her parasol beside her, and the innocent young man was sitting opposite them with his back to the cabby. At one of the squares off Sloane Street, Ford descended and left cards. Then we were off again. At the next stop Ford said he would wait outside with me. So Violet alone descended and went in.

While we were waiting, Ford said, 'You feel shy, David, but when I was your age I was so shy that I would crawl through a hedge rather than pass a labourer on the road and have to reply if he said it was a fine day. It's terrible feeling shy, but you get over it in time.'

I don't think Ford had completely got over it that afternoon. Our next port of call was off the Cromwell Road at the Sedgwicks'. We all went up to find a very smart, rather young Mrs Sedgwick, and one or two ladies and gentlemen taking tea. It was quite evident from the stares given us that the ladies had heard of Ford's connection with Violet and were somewhat surprised by his presence. Ford, I think, was unhappy. Soon Adam Sedgwick came into the room, and all my attention was focused upon him.

He was short, red-faced and stout, but there was a delightful mixture of bluntness and urbanity about him, which, if it did not set me immediately at ease (that was impossible because I was regretting having allowed myself to be taken on the idiotic expedition), gave me hope for the future. Soon he came and talked to me and led me to a window. There he inquired who Ford was, as well as asking me what knowledge of zoology I had, and saying that he looked forward to having me at his lectures. Soon afterwards Violet said goodbye, and we departed. We drove on for them to pay a call on the popular novelist Miss Netta Syrett, and for some reason I waited outside. When they came out I thanked them and went home.

I was to see more of Ford and Violet that summer. I was at a loose end till I went to the Imperial College in October, so Constance thought I could be best employed in learning German. Ford wrote to his aunt, Frau Emma Goesen, on my behalf, and she found a Prussian officer's widow, Frau Major Heider, who was glad to have me as a boarder for a month. I have never during my long life of eighty-six years, met such unpleasant people as the Heiders.

They had just satisfied themselves that I was Jewish and therefore an outcast, because my first name was David and my surname—a semi-precious stone—must be Jewish also, but the final proof was that I was reading the poems of Heine, who was, they told me, a Jew. Ford came to rescue me.

When Elsie refused to divorce him, and it became increasingly clear that Violet could not be received by the sort of people whose acquaintance she valued, Ford thought of a solution to their troubles. He was a Roman Catholic but had married Elsie in a register office. It was clear that it was no marriage. If the English law would not regard his youthful error as a valid reason for divorce, he would get one in Germany; then Violet and he would marry—and while he was persuading her, he persuaded himself that he would revive the family title and inherit the family estates. It would involve his taking up German nationality—but that should not be difficult. *Das Vaterland* would be proud to take such a distinguished son into its arms. Violet set to work on a book about herself entitled *The Desirable Alien*.

Ford could believe what he wanted to—especially if it was to his advantage. He had come to Germany with Violet to arrange the divorce and the marriage, to take up the title and German nationality—and with it the estates. He was having conferences with lawyers and dignitaries of the Church. Thus it came about that he was visiting his aunt, and that she invited me to tea.

Frau Goesen lived in a larger house with a beautiful garden, and was well above the Heiders in the social hierarchy of Boppard. As a result they looked at me with new eyes, thinking that possibly they had been mistaken. Frau Goesen would not have invited a Jewish outcast to meet *der berühmte Dichter* her nephew. . .

I tidied my hair, put on a clean collar, and went to have tea. Ford was very well dressed, kind as ever. With his fresh complexion and rabbit teeth he was an ornament to his aunt's garden, and he was quite genuinely glad to see me. So after tea, served on a smooth lawn, under a spreading tree, we said goodbye to the old lady and strolled along the bank of the Rhine to where Violet had been parked in a café. They were staying at Assmannshausen higher up the river, and before they went on board the little steamer, they invited me to visit them there.

On my return to the Heiders I was besieged with questions. Not least of which was, 'Who is the lady who waited for Ford in the café?'

According to Violet Hunt, 'two very young men, faring on foot to Switzerland—dear Dollie Radford's son and his friend David, the son of Edward and Constance Garnett. The beardless future author of *Lady Into Fox* stayed to breakfast with us and passed onwards down the Rhine.' On that visit I gave Violet a tortoise.

Apart from not faring on to Switzerland, this is probably correct. But I went again to visit them and stayed in a little hotel near their big one. After tea Ford and Violet and I climbed up to the huge Germania statue, commemorating the Franco-Prussian war. A vast Valkyrie stood brandishing her sword at the distant Vosges, from behind what she mistakenly thought was the safe barrier of the Rhine. We walked round Germania and went down to dinner. Next morning Ford and I had our photographs taken and then crossed the river and went for a stroll along the bank from Rudesheim. And Ford, in the most excellent spirits, began to tell me stories.

'My family has lived hereabouts, you know, for very many centuries, probably from the time of Charlemagne. When I was a small boy I used to go and stay with my grandmother, who lived in a house on the end of the bridge, by the fortress of Ehrenbreitstein. They used to send me upstairs to play by myself in the attics. And those attics were full of *hats*. There were hats there of every size and shape and of all periods of

DAVID GARNETT AND
FORD MADOX HUEFFER

German history—from the slashed cockscombs of the Minnesingers, right down to the eighteenth-century three-cornered hats and top hats and panamas.

'You see my family had the hereditary right to stop anyone who crossed the bridge and ask him for his hat. Bismarck put an end to it when they asked him for his. But, of course, most of the hats were military. You see the Grande Armée crossed that bridge in 1812 on the way to Russia. No wonder the attics were full of shakos!'

'Half a million of them, I suppose,' I murmured, thinking of the hatless regiments marching on to Moscow.

Ford chuckled, but decided on realism. 'No, they didn't take them all . . . they only took one from each company . . . usually the Colonel's . . . sometimes only a drummer-boy's . . . but I shall never forget those great attics full of shakos.' He dismissed the subject with a charming smile in which his mouth lost its fishy look.

A car approached, and Ford waved to it. Inside there was a gentleman who seemed surprised and startled but raised his hand a little vaguely in return.

'My dear friend Prince Metternich,' Ford explained. 'When his grandfather divided up Europe he kept the Johannisberg vineyard for himself, a couple of acres which grew the best hock in the world. The field next to it gets half an hour less sun and is only very moderate. Remind me to tell the head waiter and we'll have a bottle. . .'

I didn't remind him, and the waiter brought Rudesheimer, which was quite good enough for me at that age.

As we turned back from our stroll, I caught sight of a small raft of logs coming down the river and noticed that unlike the great pine rafts from the Black Forest on which there are houses and whole families afloat, this small affair was of beech wood. I pointed it out to Ford, who shook his head and said in melancholy tones: 'All those trees are floating down the river to ruin the digestion of the British working class.'

My look of astonishment was satisfactory, for Ford said even more lugubriously: 'Those trees are not sawn up for timber. They are distilled into acetic acid to make vinegar, of a kind guaranteed to give you a stomach-ache—only for export. It is a greater danger to the happiness of the British people than the German fleet will ever be.'

A few weeks later I was in Freiburg where I expected money. But I found a letter from Constance saying she thought I must have enough on which to return to England.

I succeeded in ringing up the hotel at Assmannshausen, but the

Manager told me that Ford and Violet had left for Bad Nauheim, but he would get in touch.

Next morning I went to the Post Office and found a hundred marks waiting for me. How I blessed Ford! I wrote at once to thank Ford and to Constance demanding my fare home. Ford's hundred marks would pay for the week walking through the Black Forest, sleeping out, on which I had set my heart.

Some time after Violet and Ford had returned to England, the *Throne* printed an account of some social occasion, stating that Mrs Ford Hueffer had been present. Elsie issued a writ, after Robert Garnett had asked her to employ another solicitor.

The editor of the *Throne* was Mr René Byles, who as director of the publisher Alston Rivers had been responsible for Ford's greatest literary success, *The Soul of London*. He had persuaded Lord Northcliffe to give it a column in the *Daily Mail*. He then went around telling editors of the other newspapers what Northcliffe had promised and so got them to do the same. He was thus a friend to whom Ford owed gratitude. On receiving a letter from Elsie's new solicitor demanding an apology and—perhaps a hundred pounds—damages, Byles went and saw Ford and Violet. They assured him that Ford had been divorced in Germany and that they had been legally married.

Both statements were lies—but on the strength of them Byles decided to fight the case. Elsie won it, and as a result of Ford's friendship, Byles had to pay out about a thousand pounds, and the *Throne* had to cease publication. Violet fled to Boulogne.

Ford and Violet went back to Germany, but when war came in August 1914 not only had the divorce, marriage, title, nationality and estates vanished, but Ford, renouncing the name of Hueffer, ceased to have German connections.

If I remember rightly, he was then of Ruthenian ancestry. He wrote some books of propaganda for his friend Masterman and enlisted. He ought to have commanded a division—but was sent back from the Front by his Colonel with a note to say he could not recommend such a perfectly useless officer even for home service. Ford had had shell-shock and was delirious in hospital. H. G. Wells believed that Ford was permanently damaged by this breakdown.

However he went on writing.

Ford was always kind to me. I liked him and am not ungrateful, though I may appear to be.

Edward Thomas

Edward Thomas

I was aged twelve when my father invited Edward and Helen Thomas for the weekend. From the first I was charmed by his beauty, though it would not have occurred to me, at that age, to use the word. Because of it I at once felt at ease with him and knew he was a friend.

He was tall, lean, with the wiry strength of a gypsy's lurcher dog. He had a high forehead with a shock of fair hair receding from it, a straight nose and questioning grey eyes under level brows. He was dressed in soft homespun tweeds and went bareheaded at a time when caps or hats were universal. Thomas walked a great deal, and always carried an ashplant stick. Almost at once we found that we had in common a love of the books of Richard Jefferies; *Bevis* and *After London* were my favourites. He was to write a book about Jefferies, and I had drawn the map of the New Sea in the just published edition of *Bevis*, for which Gerald Duckworth had sent me the princely sum of five shillings.

Helen Thomas was a short, plump, rosy-cheeked young woman wearing spectacles. They had just gone to live in a small farmhouse outside the Weald village near Sevenoaks. It was about ten miles from our cottage in the Chart woods near Limpsfield, and when they left, they invited me to walk over and spend a night with them.

This was an exciting expedition for me. I had not gone a long walk alone before. I set off that early summer morning with a packet of sandwiches, a map, and the compass that Conrad had given me. After Chartwell I was in strange country. I walked as far as possible in a bee-line from one pasture bordered with oak trees to the next, following paths and farm tracks when I could, but keeping out of the way of farmhouses and cottages. Often I stopped to study the map; sat down to eat a sandwich then pushed on. There were few landmarks after Ide Hill, and it was a relief when I came out on the road running south from the Weald village. I found the Thomases' house, and was welcomed by Helen Thomas with home-made buttered scones.

EDWARD THOMAS

GREAT FRIENDS

The little farm-house was sparsely furnished with a scrubbed deal table, rush-bottomed chairs, large china mugs—in fact it was all very rustic and cottagey. The food was to match: brown bread and butter, broad beans and milk pudding. Of course I cannot actually remember furniture or food, but that is the impression that has remained and which was characteristic of Helen Thomas and the period.

It was next morning that Edward Thomas put together a fishing-rod, dug up a tin of worms, and we set off.

Across a few fields there was a pond with black oily water shaded by tall trees. Thomas put a large pellet of paste on the hook and we settled down. After a long wait there was a bite. The float disappeared, the line tightened, the rod bent. There was a fish splashing in the water. After a few minutes Thomas landed what seemed to me a gigantic fish: a tench. It was certainly over a pound in weight—possibly a pound and a half. It was the largest fish I had ever seen taken, except a salmon in the nets at Bantam in Devon. Thomas gave me the fish, and I took it back to The Cearne next morning.

But that afternoon we went to a tiny cottage nearby, which Thomas had found for a penniless Welsh poet he had rescued from a common lodging-house in London. Thomas had read us some bits of his poems the night before. His name was W. H. Davies, and he had been a tramp in the United States where he had lost a leg trying to board a train. After that he returned to England and became a pedlar of buttons and shoelaces. He had some of his poems printed and sold them as broadsheets.

The cottage in which Thomas had installed him was almost empty. There was one chair, one table, a pail full of water and a wooden packing case. Davies was a short, dark man with eyes like stewed prunes. He had a wooden leg with a leather bucket into which his knee went and which was strapped round his thigh.

Although I had liked the poem Thomas had read, I was dismayed by Davies's appearance. His own description of himself is accurate:

> My face is large, my lips are thick,
> My skin is coarse and black almost, . . .

But I cannot agree with the next two lines:

> But the ugliest feature is my verse,
> Which proves my soul is black and lost.

The exact opposite is true. His poetry has the sweet springlike quality of such seventeenth-century poets as Herrick and Suckling.

W. H. DAVIES

painting by Sir William Nicholson

Only a few of Davies's poems had then been published. Before they brought him any return, his uncle, a poor shepherd on the Welsh hills, saw his nephew's name in print and, deciding to share in his good fortune, walked all the way from Wales to the little cottage in Kent. When he arrived he found his nephew stripped to the waist washing his only shirt and living in destitution. The old shepherd spent some time cursing Davies with every foul epithet in the Welsh language and then turned round and walked back to his mountain sheep.

Edward got to know Davies and persuaded Bernard Shaw to write an introduction to *The Autobiography of a Supertramp*. Shaw was also responsible for the title. This established Davies's reputation. Edward also got his employers to publish Davies's poems and novels. Davies moved from the Weald to Sevenoaks and used to walk over to The Cearne, a distance of eight miles, to keep himself fit. After he had achieved fame, he bought himself a cork leg, but always lamented having discarded the old peg-leg which was less tiring. Constance was a good deal amused when Davies confided to her that he was being persecuted by Society women who invited him to lunch or dinner. To Davies an invitation from a woman could only mean one thing, and he had become scared by the number of women—many of them elderly—who had suddenly begun chasing him. He did not realise that a tramp poet was a curiosity that fashionable hostesses liked to exhibit, and that he would soon be forgotten when his novelty had worn off.

The morning after my meeting with Davies I walked back to The Cearne triumphant with the huge tench, as I thought it, in my knapsack. My friendship with Thomas flourished. We met occasionally at the Mont Blanc Restaurant in Gerrard Street where Edward lunched with his writer friends on Tuesdays.

Thomas was for a time a vegetarian, and he invited me several times to have lunch with him at Eustace Miles's famous restaurant in William IV Street, where Chatto & Windus have their offices now. I call it famous because Eustace Miles was a lawn tennis champion and therefore a living proof that vegetarians could be the equals of carnivorous men.

The restaurant had also the advantage that portions of nuttered parsnips were inexpensive. The menu contained elaborate dishes such as nut cutlets dipped in egg and breadcrumbs fried in nutta, or raised pies in which meat was replaced by carrots and beetroots, and meat jelly by tapioca.

I treated these dishes with derision and contempt and made fun of Thomas for not going to the pub next door where grilled steaks and cold beef were available. He did not resent my bad manners and would either defend himself or laugh at my sallies, while he ate the nut cutlets sprinkled with plasmon powder, and I enjoyed my choice of poached eggs on a bed of spinach. I think Thomas enjoyed being teased by a schoolboy. It was typical of our friendship. No one stood less on his dignity. I was therefore encouraged to tell him exactly what I was thinking. From the first moment he treated me as an equal, and I think what was true of me was true of everyone he met whatever age, class or sex.

The Thomases moved to Steep, on the ridge above Petersfield, and my later visits were made to Berryfield Cottage. It was exceedingly narrow but otherwise much like their home at the Weald with scrubbed wood furniture, bright chintzes, large mugs and pottery. Helen Thomas was the busy, rosy-cheeked, plump mother and cottage housewife. Her husband, so quiet and thoughtful, so tall and lean, did not quite suit that setting of domestic chatter. He was more at home out of doors, though he must have spent many hours of the day in his study turning out the stream of commissioned books which kept his family cheerful and well-fed.

I was not aware of this slavery, nor did I find it strange, as Constance spent many hours every day at her writing-table, and though Edward did not write books, he sat far into the night reading and judging the books of others. I felt no deference or respect for authors. My friend was a hack writer like most other people I knew. I respected Conrad because he had been the captain of a sailing ship, Hudson because he knew every bird by sight and by its song, Nevinson and Brailsford because they had fought for the Greeks against the Turks—but nobody for being a writer. I either enjoyed a book a man wrote, or I did not. But I felt no more awe or respect than I did for a blackbird because I loved its song, or contempt than I did for a jay becaused it screeched.

On one of my visits to Steep I plunged down through a beechwood hanger where tall, white butterfly orchids were in flower, to Bedales in Petersfield, where my oldest friend, Noel Olivier, was at school, bearing an invitation to tea from Helen Thomas. I aroused suspicion and had to wait alone in a room until the headmaster's wife was free to cross-examine me. Finally I was allowed to speak to Noel for a few minutes, but she was not free that afternoon. Later, after my visit to Berryfield Cottage was over, Helen Thomas was more successful, and Noel was able to visit the Thomases several times.

On what I think was my last visit, Thomas took me for an all day walk to Selborne and beyond.

We stopped for lunch by a stile leading into a wood and as I ate my sandwiches I asked Thomas what he thought of Rupert Brooke's poems, a question which led to a discussion of contemporary poets. He put Robert Frost first. At that time Frost's poems were unknown in the United States—his first book having been published in England. Thomas got to know him and introduced him and his poems to Edward, who praised his work highly in an article in, I think, the *Atlantic Monthly*, thus helping Frost to be recognised in his native land.

Thomas greatly admired de la Mare. He thought Rupert Brooke a poet of great promise—provided he did not subside into being a university don lecturing about poetry, instead of writing it. When I mentioned the name of Gerald Gould—a critic and poet whom I knew—Thomas dismissed him. He did not care for Ezra Pound—he thought him affected, but he did not dismiss him as I had expected. He was interested to know that I had read vast quantities of Doughty, whose poetry as well as whose *Arabia Deserta* my father greatly admired. He shared Edward's admiration, though with reservations. When we had eaten our sandwiches, we went on and Thomas told me about White as we walked through Selborne.

In my youth I liked to introduce my friends to each other—which I have found a most dangerous practice, for they frequently not only disliked each other but felt contempt for my bad taste. Or else they fell in love and I lost both parties.

With Thomas I was luckier. I had introduced Noel while she was at Bedales. I now introduced Thomas to Godwin Baynes and his circle of Hampstead friends: Arnold and Clifford Bax, Joan and Bertie Farjeon and Bertie's sister, Eleanor. Meeting these younger people was a liberation for Thomas. He had been tied by the slavery of writing books, meeting newspaper editors, publishers and their readers and hack writers of all kinds—men he had to know in order to make the few pounds with which to support his family.

These new friends welcomed him. Eleanor fell in love with him and he blossomed in their society. But his greatest liberation was to come with the 1914–18 War.

He enlisted, and as an officer in the artillery he was, almost for the first time, free to write without a thought of money.

All his poetry was written in the two years before a direct hit from a German shell blew him out of existence. Those poems are read today and have given him life in the hearts of their readers.

John Galsworthy

John Galsworthy

I knew Galsworthy from 1900, when I was eight years old, until July 1914, a few days before the war, when I was twenty-two. He was brought to our cottage by Conrad, but I do not remember that visit. Soon afterwards he came to stay for a night or two. Like Conrad he wore a rimless eyeglass, which he put in his right eye when surprised by something that had been said and wanted to listen seriously. Thus he used his eyeglass more as though it were a hearing-aid than a help to sight.

In spite of impeccable clothes, knickerbockers, hand-knitted stockings and (probably) a Norfolk jacket, he could rise nobly to the occasion if there was a crisis. Our dog Pupsie, a wretched animal, dug up a sheep's head buried some weeks before and brought the stinking object, dripping with maggots, into our porch. Jack carried it away on a shovel, found a spade and buried it so deep in the garden that there could be no further resurrection. My mother was very grateful, and I impressed.

In the same practical way he dealt with the Peases' mad cat which ripped open my left eyebrow, missing the eye by half an inch. He collared her fearlessly, put her in the cat basket and accompanied by my mother carried her back to the Peases' house. We had offered the creature hospitality while they were away.

Jack was always kind and generous to me. At that age I was Lone Wolf, chief of a tribe of Red Indians of which Jack became an honorary member called Running Elk. He richly deserved the name for he had shot deer in the virgin forests of British Columbia with an Indian guide. Yet he was never an intimate who took the lead in games as Conrad had been.

After my mother and I went to live in Hampstead and I went to school in Gower Street, we fairly often called on Jack, who by then was living with Ada, more or less secretly, in Addison Road off Holland Park. Her

JOHN GALSWORTHY

hair was already going grey, and was worn *à la Pompadour*, built up above the forehead and swept back. She was like a dark flower—the title of one of Jack's bad novels. She had dark eyes, was scented and wore a lovely chinchilla fur. I think I was aware of some restraint, perhaps carefully restrained criticism of my mother's clothes.

They were made by Miss Balham, a slightly dotty active member of the Women's Freedom League, who would come to stay for two or three days, filling the study with paper patterns and the sewing machine instead of manuscripts and dictionaries. Even after making all allowances for Miss Balham's advanced political views, Ada, probably dressed by Paquin or Worth, found her handiwork embarrassing.

Ada was musical, and she composed the settings for some of Jack's poems. I remember her singing one called *Straw in the Street*. As the title conveys nothing to readers born since rubber tyres replaced horseshoes, I must explain. When someone living in one of the upper-class houses in the West End was seriously ill or dying, the street would be covered deep in straw for a distance of perhaps twenty yards on each side of it to deaden the clatter of horses' hoofs. The theme of Jack's song was therefore that there is suffering even in the houses of the rich—for death comes to rich and poor alike.

Jack and Ada invited us to concerts occasionally. At one of them we arrived early and Ada took off her hat and pinned it with a long hatpin to the back of an empty seat in front of her. Just as the concert was starting a portly gentleman plopped down into it and uttered a cry. He had leant back against Ada's hatpin. He went off and did not return until the interval when he reproved her with the words: 'You might have caused my instant death.'

Jack and Ada were all apologies and concern, but Constance and I had difficulty in keeping our faces, for his words struck us as ludicrous. The phrase became one of my mother's favourites.

When I was about sixteen Jack led me up to the landing on the stairs at Addison Road and opened a cabinet containing two shot-guns and a rifle. One of the shot-guns, though a twelve-bore, had shorter barrels and was much lighter than the other. It had silvery Damascus barrels, and I fell in love with it at sight. Jack was actually saying, 'Which would you choose?' But before I could speak he added, 'But I shall give you the rifle.'

It was impossible for me to say, 'I would rather have the little shot-gun,' for I saw that he had repented of asking me to choose.

He took out the rifle and handed it to me, and I thanked him. It was a splendid gift—but, oh! for that shot-gun. It was before Churchill started making XXVs with steel barrels, so I suppose it was a lady's gun made by Purdey.

The rifle was a Colt 320 which Jack had bought to shoot deer in British Columbia. The magazine—it was a repeater—was in a long tube below the barrel. When it was full the end was heavy, and the weight and point of balance shifted every time you fired a cartridge. It was fairly accurate up to about thirty yards, but the English .32 cartridges we bought were not a perfect fit. So, though I was immensely proud of owning a rifle, I was secretly bitterly disappointed. He gave me books also at appropriate seasons.

I think Constance and I were tolerated by Ada because Edward was Jack's literary mentor, and it was Constance's translations which had led Jack to write and to get to know us.

After Ada's divorce, the Galsworthys were able to come out of hiding and moved to Holly Lodge, a fine house with a lovely garden in Hampstead.

We were at that time extremely hard up, and one or two of the admirers of Constance's translations combined in secret to obtain a Civil List pension for her. When Edward heard of this he was furious and wrote angrily to the originators of the plan. Galsworthy and, I think, Arnold Bennett were the chief culprits. But Jack argued and wrote, and finally got Edward to see that he was behaving selfishly and unreasonably, so the pension was accepted. When my mother's translations of Tchehov's stories and plays began to bring in money, she resigned the pension.

Some time after that, Jack and Ada established themselves at Manaton on the edge of Dartmoor. Jack was in any case a 'Man of Devon'. By then Ada had shown that she preferred Nellie Heath (with whom my father had a permanent liaison from about 1898 until his death in 1937) to Constance, and while Edward and Nellie were invited to Manaton, Constance and I were not.

Actually my father had lost all interest in Jack's writing after he became a best-selling author and playwright. But their friendship was never broken. Constance may have wounded Jack's pride by writing to thank him for sending her one of the later books—possibly *The White Monkey*—and telling him that he wrote too much and must be more critical of his work. He had replied justifying himself by saying that he was supporting so many humanitarian causes.

The last time I saw Jack and Ada was at Manaton. It was the end of July, or the first days of August 1914. I had been camping at St Feoch on Falmouth Harbour and had met a friend of my uncle Arthur Garnett, Charles Dear, who was living in a houseboat with wife Lil, their baby and a New Forest gypsy girl of seventeen called Ann Witcher. She was there to look after the baby and help Lil with the housework. Ann was fair for a gypsy, marvellously strong and healthy and always enjoyed the baby and was gay and gentle with it. I think that she was illiterate, but that Lil had inspired her with the wish to learn to read and write.

Charles Dear had been a rich young man when at Cambridge, but had dissipated his fortune on horses, hounds and fox-hunting. He had then taken up painting landscapes. I thought his work had no merit.

They left Cornwall before I did and invited me to join them where they were camping in a horse caravan above Becka Falls on Dartmoor. When the time came I walked the hundred miles there by way of the coast, in four days, carrying my camping equipment and cooking my own food.

Soon after I turned up, when we were all in the van, for it was raining, Charles Dear said mischievously, 'We shall have some peace now you've come.'

And Lil explained, 'Ann has been asking every hour of the day when you were going to arrive.'

Ann jumped up, and crying, 'You pair of devils, man and woman,' rushed out into the rain.

When I spoke a few days later of going to call on the Galsworthys both Charles and Lil said, 'You ought to take Ann with you.'

I did not want to, but Ann was very keen to come, so I took her. I had written to say that I was camping at Becka Falls and had been invited to tea.

Ann spent the whole morning in the stream above the Falls where it is hidden in a wood, scrubbing herself (though she was always quite clean) and putting on her best dress.

It was a frightful little ill-fitting coat and skirt of a bright blue that screamed at one.

Ann's appearance must have startled Ada, but the girl behaved with composure. Soon a maid in a white cap brought in a tray of tea and plates of little sandwiches. As soon as it was possible, Jack said he would like to show me the house and the stables, and we walked round and I admired two lovely riding horses.

We talked chiefly about the fate of some of the balloons in the Gordon-Bennett Balloon Race. Some had got into Central Europe,

ANN WITCHER
WITH MRS DEAR AND HER BABY

some only to Holland, but one or two were missing. It seemed more important than the prospect of war with Germany, though the postman, a naval reservist, had been called up.

Meanwhile Ann had been left with Ada, who I am sure was kind. Ann had been thrilled by the visit. She had never been inside a private house before, she had never been where there were servants, she had never sat talking to a lady in her drawing-room. So she had plenty to think over. However we walked back in silence until she said suddenly:

'My Auntie's name is Faith, Hope and Charity.'

It seemed an appropriate remark.

I was glad I had taken Ann. I had, I knew, 'torn it' as far as I was concerned, but I had also torn away the pretence that Jack and Ada had escaped being conventionally-minded members of their class.

I felt certain that they believed that I was having an affair with Ann and had been shocked and thought ill of me on that account.

Actually Ann and I had never kissed or even held hands though I think we should both have liked to. But it was impossible because the Dears were looking on.

Ann sometimes surprised me. Once when I had crawled out of my lightweight tent when it was raining, and a soft wind was blowing the mist and the rain among the trees, I found Ann standing in the doorway of the bell tent where she slept.

'What are you doing, Ann?' I asked.

'I'se watching the rain. It's beautiful.'

She was protected by the flap of her tent from being soaked by the rain, but she was letting its beauty soak into her for an hour or more. Any of my friends would have glanced at it for a few seconds, and said, 'Oh, how lovely,' and gone on to something else.

I set out to write about Jack and Ada, and I am writing about a gypsy girl. My excuse is the contrast. The contrast between the natural and real and instinctive, and the cultured striving after the good and beautiful.

Edward once told Jack that he looked at life through the windows of his club. It wasn't true when he said it, but it became true later on.

When I came back from France in the beginning of 1916 and decided to resist the conscription act, Constance wrote to Jack asking him to write a letter that could be shown to the Tribunal to say that my conscientious objection was genuine. He very rightly refused. I was glad to be sponsored by Maynard Keynes, a friend I had made for myself and who knew me, and not by an old friend of my parents who didn't.

D. H. Lawrence and Frieda

D. H. Lawrence and Frieda

Ford Madox Hueffer discovered Lawrence when Jessie Chambers, his first sweetheart, sent some of his poems to the *English Review*. These were followed by short stories, and Lawrence blossomed out in the front of the *English Review* and attracted a lot of notice. Ford then helped Lawrence to get his first novel *The White Peacock* published by Heinemann.

'Ford was the kindest of men,' Lawrence wrote—and one is glad to have it stated. He sent off his protégé to a good start. But Lawrence had a keen sense of the ridiculous, and Ford's omniscient and patronising manner—'olympian' Conrad called it—tickled his sense of humour. He was a brilliant mimic, and Ford was included in his repertory. Perhaps Ford sensed the irreverence. At any rate he said that Lawrence bored him.

Lawrence wrote: 'Hueffer left me to paddle my own canoe. I very nearly wrecked it and did for myself. Garnett rescued me.' The rescue took the form of inviting the young schoolmaster down from Croydon, twelve miles away, to The Cearne for weekends, reading his stories and poems, acting as his unpaid literary agent by placing his stories wherever he had influence, and becoming the confidant who was told all his love affairs. Lawrence was writing *The Trespasser* based on her love story, confided to him by Helen Corke, a fellow schoolteacher.

His rescuer very nearly killed him. One bitterly cold winter's day he went and stood by the woodpile while Edward was splitting logs with wedges and beetle and cutting them to manageable size with the axe. It was a pleasure to watch him, but Lawrence got chilled to the bone, and on his return to Croydon went down with pneumonia.

After his illness, he visited his home town of Nottingham and the miner's son, having increased his status in Professor Weekley's eyes by having become a schoolmaster, was invited to his house. Frieda was Mrs Weekley. Lawrence and she fell in love at first sight. She was brought to

D. H. LAWRENCE IN 1913

The Cearne, and soon afterwards they departed for Germany. Frieda's father, Baron von Richthofen, held an important post at Metz, and they went there, but later moved to the valley of the Isar, where at first they slept in adjacent villages.

In July 1912, I was spending some weeks alone in Munich. I knew no one, and it promised a pleasant change when Edward wrote suggesting that I should meet the author of *The White Peacock*. On the heels of his letter came one from Lawrence inviting me to come out and see him, and adding, in a postscript, 'I look fearfully English, and so I guess do you, so there is no need for either of us to carry the Union Jack for recognition.'

The bare-headed, slight figure that moved towards me on the platform at Icking did look fearfully English. I noticed a scrubby little moustache, and I was looking into the most beautiful lively blue eyes. Lawrence was slight in build, with a weak, narrow chest and shoulders, but he was a good height and very light in his movements. This lightness gave him a sort of grace. His hair was mud-colour with a streak of red in it, a thick mat, parted on one side. His forehead was broad but not high, his nose was short and lumpy, his face colourless like a red-haired man's, his chin (he had not then adopted a beard) round like a hairpin—a Philip IV chin, the lower lip red and moist under the scrubby toothbrush moustache. He looked like a mongrel terrier among the crowd of German Alsatians and Pomeranians, English to the bone. You could find him in every gang of workmen, the man who keeps the others laughing all the time, who makes trouble with the boss, and who is saucy to the foreman, who gets the sack, who is 'victimised' and is the cause of a strike, and is always cocky, cheeky and in trouble.

He was all this, but once you looked into his eyes you were completely charmed, they were so alive, dancing with gaiety. His smile lit up all his face as he looked at you, asking you silently: 'Come on—let's have some fun.'

No doubt Lawrence made me talk about myself as we walked from Icking to Irschenhausen and then into the woods, where he said there were roe deer. In the afternoon we walked further down the valley through a forest by the river's edge. *Osmunda regalis* was growing in the shadow of the trees, and the river tore past the rocks and the white sandbanks. I bathed, and we went on to Wolfratshausen, where Lawrence led me into an orchard behind the house and introduced me to Frieda. Her head and the whole carriage of her sturdy body were noble.

FRIEDA AND MONTAGUE WEEKLEY
TEN YEARS BEFORE SHE MET LAWRENCE

Her eyes were green with a lot of tawny yellow in them, the nose straight. She looked me dead in the eyes, judging me, and at that moment she was like a lioness, eyes, nose, and colouring and the swift power of her lazy leap up from the hammock where she had been lying. She was, as Lawrence had written to Edward, 'ripping' and 'the woman of a lifetime'. I have always been attracted by happy lovers and Lawrence and Frieda were more than twice as attractive to me together than they would have been separately. I was completely charmed by each of them, and at once worshipped them. I was at a worshipping stage anyway. However if anybody was to be worshipped, I was quite right to fix on them. They were worthy.

GREAT FRIENDS

They on their part flattered me, buttered me up, laughed at me and became fond of me, accepting my worship and lecturing me for worshipping other people. After that first visit they asked me again several times, introduced me to Frieda's sister and brother-in-law, and in a week or so I was at home in a new family circle.

There was a bad moment in the day—when the post came from England, for Frieda's husband, Professor Weekley, wrote by nearly every post. If the address were in his handwriting, Frieda would hand the letter to Lawrence and say 'See what he says. . .' Then Lawrence would tear the envelope open and read it aloud. A jealous man always appears in a poor light. But Ernest Weekley's letters revealed the very worst and most contemptible side of his character. There was a stream of invective about Lawrence, and then appeals to Frieda's better instincts. How could she so demean herself as to elope with a miner's son? With a man who was not a gentleman? What would his friends in Nottingham be saying when they learned that she had so betrayed her birth and upbringing?

'Ernst is not so very grand himself', Frieda exclaimed, as Lawrence finished the letter and threw it aside. 'To think that I was married for twelve years—yes, for twelve years—to a man who cares only what his neighbours will think! And do you know why I married him? I had been reading Tennyson, and I thought Ernst was Lancelot! Our marriage started badly. I went to the bedroom first and climbed up by the door, and when Ernst came in, I threw myself naked into his arms. He was horrified and told me to put on my nightdress at once. Can you imagine such a man? And he wants me to go back and live with him for fear of what his neighbours in Nottingham will say when they find out I have run away with a miner's son!'

After they had packed up and gone to the Tyrol, planning to make their way by stages into Italy, letters and messages reached me telling me that I must join them at Mayrhofen in Zillerthal—the wild flowers in the mountains were wonderful, and I should make great additions to my herbarium. I was a student of botany at that time.

Leaving a note for Harold, an old friend whom I was expecting in Munich, to follow by train, I set off to walk by Achensee to Mayrhofen, where I took a room in a house across the street from the Lawrences. There was an oleander in flower before the door, and strings of mules with red tassels loaded with huge Emmenthal cheeses were coming down the village street out of the mountains.

Lawrence pointed everything out: he knew everyone in the village by

78

name and all their peculiarities and love affairs. Frieda and he had been there nearly a week.

He was just finishing writing *Sons and Lovers* and was writing stories and a lot of poems, but his writing did not affect our daily life. It never occurred to me, or I think to Frieda, not to interrupt him, and we spent all day together in one room, while he scribbled away in the corner, jumping up continually to look after the cooking. Scratch, scratch, scratch, went his pen on the squared foreign paper; then scratch, scratch, with the penholder at the back of his low-class head of hair. Scratch on the paper again—and then Lawrence would jump up and begin to make fun of himself, or else Frieda was bubbling over with some new thing that she had seen out of the window, or else the soup was burning.

Lawrence was a natural copy-cat. Indeed he was the only great mimic I have ever known. The slightest affectation of manner, or social pretence, was seized on mercilessly. I realised the enjoyment which the poor are offered by the spectacle of the imbecilities of the rich—of the endless 'copy' they provided to their servants. But the person Lawrence most often made fun of was himself.

He mimicked himself ruthlessly, and as he told a story acted versions of a shy and gawky Lawrence being patronised by literary lions, or a winsome Lawrence charming his landlady, a sentimental Lawrence being put in his place by his landlady's daughter, or a whining Lawrence picking a quarrel with Frieda over nothing.

In the evening we acted complicated nonsense charades, without an audience. For years after, Frieda would ask me when we met, 'Do you remember, David, the head of Holofernes?' and then collapse with laughter, and explain: 'Oh! You looked such a fool!' Lawrence's high spirits kept us all gay. His courage and mockery of the slightest hint of self-pity rose with danger and difficulty. And at that time their difficulties were very great. But what did they matter? He was walking to Italy with the woman he loved.

Lawrence and Frieda set off for Italy with twenty-three pounds between them and with no certainty of any more until *Paul Morel* was published, and *Paul Morel* was being rewritten and transformed into *Sons and Lovers*. About money Lawrence was scrupulous, extremely economical and always ready to give it away. At Mayrhofen Lawrence offered to lend me the money to accompany them into Italy, from which I could return by boat from Genoa. Though much tempted, I refused, and have regretted doing so ever since.

GREAT FRIENDS

After I had been a few days at Mayrhofen, Harold joined us. Lawrence and Frieda sent off all their possessions in two suitcases by train to Italy, and we set off to walk over the mountains rising up through the wet forests, with their yellow foxgloves and *noli-me-tangere* flowers, to the rocky pastures where the trees stopped, and the belt of *Alpenrosen*, dwarf rhododendrons, began.

Lawrence wrote two stories about our walk: *A Chapel Among the Mountains* and *A Hay Hut Among the Mountains*. Rain had come on, and towards evening we found the hayhut and bedded down in it for the night, and there was a most violent thunderstorm with flashes that lit up the stalks of hay where we nestled. When we looked out in the morning the snow had come down to the lower slopes.

But the sun shone hot next day, and Harold and I were glad to stop and bathe in the torrents of ice-water rushing from the glaciers above. Every few yards Lawrence or I would find some new flower and tear it up by the roots to add to my herbarium, which was enriched, in three days, by nearly two hundred Alpine species. Lawrence loved flowers, which play a large part in his symbolism and personal mythology.

At the end of our second day's walk, Lawrence and I climbed up a wild tumbled scree of rocks almost to the permanent snow-line, snatching at the saxifrages that we found, while Harold and Frieda stayed behind at the Dominikus Hutte, where my companion was, no doubt most willingly, seduced. Frieda did not tell Lawrence about this until we had gone. It was not the first event of the kind since their elopement. After they had had a violent scene at Irschenhausen, Frieda ran down to the river, swam across it and made love to a woodcutter working on the far side. Anna Wickham wrote a poem about it, after I had told her the story.

Next morning we all crossed the Pfitzer Joch and descended the mountainside, which is cut into steps like a steep flight of stairs. In an hour or two, we had passed from drifted snow to houses where the grapes hung in black clusters over the lintels, and a tobacco harvest stood drying in the gardens.

Lawrence came for part of the way when Harold and I walked on to catch the Verona night express at Sterzen. When we stopped and said goodbye, he said something about not needing me to repay the money I had borrowed for my fare home. It was dark, there was a smell of flowers, and Lawrence's light feet were noiseless in the dust of the road. I never saw him so well or so happy, so consistently gay and light-hearted as he was then.

D. H. LAWRENCE AND FRIEDA

The Garnett family saw a good deal of Lawrence and Frieda during the next two years. When they came to England The Cearne was their first resting-place, for they knew that they were welcome and could stay until they had decided on their plans, or were invited elsewhere.

Harold had been out to stay with them in Italy—a somewhat rowdy visit to judge by the rude words Lawrence scribbled across a letter that Frieda wrote me.

During a walk through the Chart Woods, Lawrence told me about Frieda's seduction of Harold at the Dominikus Hutte—Harold had never hinted at it. And then Lawrence took my breath away with the words, 'Harold is no gentleman.' He might have been quoting from one of Ernest Weekley's letters.

That was in the summer of 1913—a hot one. The four Olivier girls, Harold and I had formed the habit of sleeping out in the wood under a huge Scotch pine, where there was an open space carpeted with pine-needles and none of the dreaded horse ants. Frieda and I went there one hot afternoon, and we lay down on the warm pine-needles. There was the smell of the resinous branches. We lay close to each other. Presently Frieda smiled at me and suggested that we should make love. It was the natural thing to do. I longed for the moment when. . .

But I had the strength to refuse. She and Lawrence were staying at The Cearne. I knew what Lawrence felt about Harold and that Frieda was far too outspoken to keep her mouth shut. If I yielded the situation would be impossible. I think I said all that and Frieda did not like me any the less for playing Joseph.

They enjoyed staying at the Cearne and Lawrence wrote a poem about making love to Frieda at the bottom of our apple orchard. But there were bad moments. Frieda longed to see her three children, and her love provoked Lawrence's jealousy and brought out a mean, contemptible streak in him. Once she spoke of trying to see them, and Lawrence began to nag at her until she was in tears. I witnessed this, and it was not a pleasant sight.

Frieda still clung to some of her aristocratic trappings: her pride in being a *Freifräulein*—a more appropriate title for her than its equivalent *Baronin*—was exhibited in her beautiful cambric linen handkerchiefs embroidered with a coronet in the corner. I coveted one, and when I saw one of them crumpled up, dropped outside the bedroom door, I picked it up and quickly dropped it again. It contained sputum and was brightly stained with arterial blood. Lawrence already had tuberculosis.

GREAT FRIENDS

In the winter, Constance went out and stayed in a hotel close to where they were living on the gulf of Spezia. It was about then that Edward told me that he had a mass of Lawrence's poems, and asked me to select the ones I liked best, to be published in his first volume of poems. I was young and reading a great deal of poetry, and I should judge them with a fresh eye. Edward accepted my choice, though he added one or two poems in dialect which I did not care for. My only regret is that there was no copy of *Snapdragon* among those I chose from. It is perhaps the finest of his early love poems. It was published soon afterwards by Eddie Marsh in *Georgian Poetry*. In other respects I think that *Love Poems and Others* is a good selection.

Frieda's son, Monty, was at St Paul's School, and she decided to try and intercept him as he was leaving the building. Lawrence tried to stop her going and refused to accompany her, so I went with her. We waited on the pavement opposite the school gate. At length the boy came out. Frieda ran across and greeted him. But Monty was scared. He had been told he must not speak of his mother, or think of her, and he knew that meeting her would be forbidden. He was embarrassed and soon escaped, and I led Frieda away sobbing after this shattering experience.

Lawrence and Frieda were in England in the summer of 1914. I went back to the Imperial College before term had started, and was delighted to find that they were living near by in a little house lent them by James Campbell (Lord Glenavy) just off the Fulham Road. Professor Weekley had divorced Frieda, and she and Lawrence had just got married.

Soon after war had broken out I invited them to come and have dinner at Pond Place to meet H. G. Newth, a demonstrator in zoology, and my best friend at the college. Edward was away, but I made free with a bottle of his Beaune. Edward's flat, or rather maisonette, was the top half of a hideous building, reached by a narrow staircase. The rooms of the tenants below stank of pet dog and of fish stewed in vinegar.

My choice of Newth was fortunate: Lawrence liked him at once, and he recalled the friends he had had when he was a schoolmaster at Croydon. My friend was a small, dark, long-headed man, what the anthropologists of that period called the Iberian type. His two gods were Samuel Butler and Schumann, and he had a habit of imitating the bark of a sea-lion.

Frieda was warm and expansive, and when we had finished our meal she talked about the war and her divided sympathies. As a young girl she had lived at the Prussian Court, and she and her sisters loathed the

D. H. LAWRENCE AND FRIEDA

Kaiser and used to run and hide in the bushes at the bottom of the garden when he was about. She believed that he personally had produced the atmosphere which made war probable. But she loved and admired her two cousins, the Von Richthofens, who had joined the German Air Force and who became its greatest tactical leaders. She loved her fashionable younger sister who had married the Crown Prince's aide-de-camp.

And now, with English children and committed by ties of love to England, she found herself being cold-shouldered because of her German origin. We listened in sympathy. Lawrence was at his sweetest and gentlest. Finally, about midnight, when they said goodbye, Newth who stayed behind to discuss them and help me wash up, called down the odoriferous staircase in his most guttural accents: '*Auf wiedersehen, gnädige Baronin!*' And Frieda called back in German.

Two or three days later, two men pushed their way into the flat and said they had come from the police to make enquiries. They didn't look like detectives, and I asked them for their cards, which I noticed had only been issued a few days before. They wanted to know how many Germans were living in our flat and who were its inhabitants. It took me some time to get rid of them. Two days later there was a visit from another pair of the same type. A week later another visit. This time it was a professional, and I asked him to strike my name off the list of suspected German spies; he laughed and said he would do his best to prevent me being worried again. I think that he told our neighbours downstairs to stop making denunciations, and I was not bothered again.

But the persecution of Lawrence and Frieda had begun, and was to last in different forms all through the war and after it.

Gilbert Cannan found them a cottage, called The Triangle, near where he lived in Buckinghamshire, and I took Francis Birrell down to see them there. Frieda and Frankie liked each other at once and began a conversation about all the people he had known in Berlin, many of whom were acquaintances or friends of Frieda's. This annoyed Lawrence, who become more and more sulky, and I realised that at any moment he might make an unpleasant scene. We were spared the explosion by the arrival of two Slade students, a girl called Carrington and Mark Gertler. The room was tiny. Frankie had appropriated the only comfortable chair, Frieda sat on the edge of the table, Lawrence was busy at the stove cooking spaghetti, Mark Gertler remained standing, and Carrington sat on the floor. The room was charged with emotion. Lawrence liked Gertler, but was annoyed at being baulked of his scene. Gertler and

Frankie were talkers, and each expected to hold the floor. Frieda was angry with Lawrence, and I had fallen in love with Carrington at first sight and taken a violent dislike to Gertler. I knew that a science student had no chance against a painter. I wished both Gertler and Frankie were at the bottom of the sea. Our visit was obviously a disaster, and how could I manage to see this blue-eyed, apple-blossom girl ever again? I guessed that she was unaware of my existence, but in this I later discovered I was wrong. She had been a good deal attracted by me. When darkness had set in we went back to London.

Soon after that visit I was invited for a weekend by Gilbert and Mary Cannan, and once again I was being violently attracted by a beautiful woman. This time it was Katherine Mansfield who was staying with Middleton Murry in another tiny cottage close by. Lawrence and Frieda came over, and we all went for a country walk together with Nana, who was much the greatest literary celebrity present. For when Gilbert Cannan had gone off with J. M. Barrie's wife, she had taken the sheepdog with her—the original Nana of *Peter Pan*. Katherine never gave a glance in my direction. Murry and she and Lawrence were talking in a group, Frieda and Gilbert had paired off and Mary Cannan, Nana and I brought up the rear.

Lawrence had changed a lot. He was rapidly growing away from Edward. Murry and Lawrence were planning *The Signature*, which ran to three numbers. Lawrence contributed *The Crown*, a symbolic effusion: The Spirit, Light, is fighting the Flesh, Darkness, like the Lion and Unicorn. It is a work of which I could not make head nor tail and the theme of which seems to me to be outworn nonsense. For me the Flesh and the Spirit are one.

Murry contributed an autobiographical fragment, and Katherine a story. When expressed in prose Lawrence's dogmatic, mystical outpourings seem to me rubbish, but they become full of mysterious significance in his poetry. Fortunately the artist in Lawrence continually flashes out. But the overt 'philosophising' mars very much of his writing, and is often unintentionally comic. For instance in *Reflections on the Death of a Porcupine* he kills a porcupine and sets out to make a statement about the hierarchical place in nature of living things. It is not Darwin, but a vague memory of Haeckel. There is absolute nonsense about the progress of 'higher' from 'lower' organisms. And with this curious ignorant dogmatism, is mixed a mystical sun-worship. And, since strong words are needed, his reflections are so much rot. But in the same volume you get *The Spinner and the Monks*, which is lovely and observant, full of love and intuitive understanding, with scarcely a dogmatic or stupid statement.

With Lawrence one must pick and choose, and discard the rubbish. I was to listen to a lot of rubbish in the early part of 1915.

It must have been about then that I introduced Lawrence to that under-rated poet, Anna Wickham. They liked each other, and when Lawrence was living in the Vale of Health, they went for walks on Hampstead Heath. Once that winter Anna's small sons danced around them snowballing Lawrence, of whom they were jealous. I wonder if she told him that her poem, *Imperatrix*, was written about one of Frieda's infidelities of which I had told her?

One Thursday, early in 1915, I had dinner at Lady Ottoline Morrell's. I sat next to Frieda and enjoyed talking to her. Lawrence was sitting next to Forster, and they were deep in conversation. Duncan Grant was there, and so were two girls from the Slade School of Art: Barbara Hiles (later Bagenal) and Carrington. During the inspirational dancing afterwards I received a violent blow in the eye from the top of Barbara's head and had a black, partially closed eye in the days which followed.

Next day I went to tea at Duncan's studio. Forster, Lawrence and Frieda were already there—Lawrence having asked to see Duncan's pictures. One after another the canvases were placed on the easel, and Lawrence delivered a tirade. Each of them was worse than the last one. While Lawrence held forth, Duncan sat rocking himself on a chair in silence. When it ended, he rose and put another picture on the stand. I noticed a look of pain on Forster's face, and very soon he slipped away. 'I must catch the train to Weybridge,' was his habitual excuse for leaving a gathering where he was unhappy.

The show and the tirade went on. It was not that the pictures were badly painted. They were misconceived. Duncan was doing the wrong thing. He must learn to look at the art of painting anew.

Occasionally Frieda made some clumsy remark, such as, 'Oh, but we liked that portrait,' to which no one paid attention. Finally Duncan and I held up two sticks, and, one winding and the other unwinding, displayed what in Duncan's obituary is described as 'an essay in kinetic abstract art'. It was bought by the Tate Gallery in 1973.

The dark, dour and silent figure of Koteliansky, one of Lawrence's disciples, arrived to fetch away Lawrence and Frieda and bring the disastrous private view to an end. Lady Ottoline loved Duncan and his work, and Lawrence wrote her a letter to explain what was wrong with it, and saying that he should 'gather up the instances of Rembrandt, Corot, Goya and Manet into an abstract whole'. Gosh!

But though Duncan failed to take advantage of Lawrence's advice, the visit bore fruit in that passage in *Lady Chatterley's Lover* in which the gamekeeper hero is taken to the studio of Duncan Forbes, who had a weird Celtic conceit of himself', and 'whose art was all tubes and valves and spirals, and strange colours ultra-modern, yet with a certain power, even a certain purity of form and tone: only Mellors thought it cruel and repellent.'

Undeterred by our visit to The Triangle, Frankie Birrell and I accepted an invitation from Lawrence to spend a weekend with them in the cottage at Greatham which had been lent them by Viola Meynell. We arrived on Saturday evening, and after supper were taken round to see the Meynells and Saleebies. Next morning Frankie and I went to breakfast with them. Wilfred Meynell, the Patriarch, was rustling the pages of the *Observer*, the room was full of dark, madonna-like girls and women, the Poetess lay stretched upon a couch, and there was the question, to which I felt instinctively that a painful answer was expected: 'Where is Francis?'

No one could say, but just before we finished our eggs and bacon, a tall handsome young man came eagerly into the room. It was Francis Meynell, who had run three miles across the marsh to mass with the Holy Fathers (or Brothers) at Amberley. With what benign and holy joy did his parents look upon him then! And how like a Blake engraving was the whole religious family at that moment! Little did I suspect that within a few years he would be a Communist smuggling Romanov jewels into England in order to finance the *Daily Herald*!

Our day passed pleasantly picnicking with old friends who were guests of the Meynells, who departed in the evening for London. I wish that we had done so also, for at supper Frankie talked and talked, and I talked, and Frieda laughed a lot. But I became aware that something dreadful was going on inside Lawrence. He was in the throes of some dark crisis and seem to shrink in size, summoning all his powers. His muscles knotted—but he said nothing. Frieda had also observed what was going on. I said that I was tired and had a long day's walk in front of me, and we retired early to bed.

There was angry and incessant whispering from the bedroom next to mine. At last the sinister sounds stopped, and I went to sleep. In the middle of the night I was woken by a series of bangs and tumbles and strangulated noises. Some one was blundering against my door. I lit a

FRANCIS BIRRELL

candle. Frankie was standing outside, swathed in thick flannel pyjamas, dumb and in great distress. By the light of the candle I saw that his mouth was choked with a large object. His tongue had swollen to enormous size. When I shoved the handle of my toothbrush into his mouth he gave nasal moans. Frieda and Lawrence came out and stared at us in astonishment. Frieda and I discussed poultices, fomentations

87

and doctors. I discovered that his temperature was normal. Frieda held a candle, and I tortured Frankie by inserting teaspoonfuls of nearly boiling water into his mouth. Then we packed him off to bed and he was glad to escape from us. I hoped that he would last till next day when I could take him to a doctor. Throughout this remarkable scene there was a quiet triumphant certainty in Lawrence's manner. He had prayed for deliverance to the Dark Gods, and they had blasted his enemy in what had seemed his strongest organ. But I think it possible that he may also have put some fantastic sexual explanation upon the incident, based perhaps on finding us in our pyjamas in the passage between our bedrooms in the early hours.

Next morning Frankie was perfectly well, and his tongue had resumed its normal functions. But Lawrence wrote me a letter:

> Greatham, Pulborough, Sussex.
> Monday.

My dear David,

I can't bear to think of you, David, so wretched as you are and your hand shaky—and everything wrong. It is foolish of you to say it doesn't matter either way—the men loving men. It doesn't matter in the public way. But it matters so much David, to the man himself—at any rate to us northern nations—that it is like a blow of triumphant decay, when I meet Birrell and the others. I simply can't bear it. It is so wrong, it is unbearable. It makes a form of inward corruption which truly makes me scarce able to live. Why is there this horrible sense of frowstiness, so repulsive, as if it came from a deep inward dirt—a sort of sewer—deep in men like K and B & D G. It is something almost unbearable to me. And not from any moral disapprobation. I myself never considered Plato very wrong, or Oscar Wilde. I never knew what it meant till I saw K., till I saw him at Cambridge. We went into his rooms at midday, and it was very sunny. He was not there, so Russell was writing a note. Then suddenly a door opened and K. was there, blinking from sleep, standing in his pyjamas. And as he stood there gradually a knowledge passed into me, which has been like a little madness to me ever since. And it was carried along with the most dreadful sense of repulsiveness—something like carrion—a vulture gives me the same feeling. I begin to feel mad as I think if it—insane.

Never bring B. to see me any more. There is something nasty about him, like black-beetles. He is horrible and unclean. I feel as if I should go mad, if I think of your set, D.G. and K. and B. It makes me dream of beetles. In Cambridge I had a similar dream. Somehow I can't bear it. It is wrong beyond all bounds of wrongness. I had felt it slightly before, in the Stracheys. But it came full upon me in K., and in D.G. And yesterday I knew it again, in B.

David, my dear, I love your father and I love your mother. I think your father has been shamefully treated at the hands of life. Though I don't see him,

D. H. LAWRENCE AND FRIEDA

I do love him in my soul—more even than I love your mother. And I feel, because he is your father, that you must leave these 'friends', these beetles. You must wrench away and start a new life. B and D.G. are done for, I think—done for for ever. K. I am not sure. But you, my dear, you can be all right. You can come away, and grow whole, and love a woman, and marry her, and make life good, and be happy. Now David, in the name of everything that is called love, leave this set and stop this blasphemy against love. It isn't that I speak from a moral code. Truly I didn't know it was wrong, till I saw K. that morning in Cambridge. It was one of the crises in my life. It sent me mad with misery and hostility and rage. Go away, David, and try to love a woman. My God, I could kiss Eleanor Farjeon with my body and soul, when I think how good she is, in comparison. But the Oliviers, and such girls, are wrong.

I could sit and howl in a corner like a child, I feel so bad about it all.

D. H. Lawrence

With this came a letter from Frieda to which Lawrence had added:

My dear David,

Don't marry anybody. Go right away and be alone and work, and come to your real self. But do leave this group of 'friends'. You have always known the wrong people—Harolds, and Olivier girls. Do go right away, right away, and be by yourself.

Love

D. H. Lawrence

Frieda's letter was as follows:

My dear David,

Are you getting sick of being bombarded with letters? I was so very fond of you when you were here, and I did not think you were satisfied or happy—I felt a great strength and livingness and a genuine *you*, if only you could *believe* in yourself more, in the individual bottomself of you and collect your strength and direct it—You always admire people much too much, you are really *more* than Birrell and the others, I *know*. But you daren't trust yourself.—I thought Ruth rather fine *for another man*—She is much too fixed in her morality, she would be your conscience-keeper and you would always want to be free—Don't marry her, David, I can see so plainly, what would happen. She would not *see* so much, that is in you and make you to ordinary tight standards. You would never come very close to her and you do want and need intimacy—And at present your vital interest is in men, just like your devotion to the Indian, but you lose and forget *yourself* in other men and you have got it in you to stand for yourself and by yourself—Also I rather think the young men you know exploit you and feed on your warmth, because you are generous—I have learnt a great deal how much one has to use one's wits, and it is want of courage if we don't stick to the self that God has given us—I think that Anna you loved, but there was something hopeless from the beginning, that has left a lot of unbelief in you—But you do really want so much and much will come, if you only let it—Anyhow, you are my dear friend,

Yours Frieda

Lawrence's letter upset me, frightened me and made me very angry. I was frightened because my friends were homosexuals, and I thought that if Lawrence went on talking like that, it might lead to prosecution, or do their reputations harm.

But Lawrence's letter made me very angry for his daring to tell me that I had always known the wrong people, and for instancing the four Olivier girls, who had been my playmates since I was four years old. I loved Noel Olivier more than I could have loved any sister; we were bound together by all the ties of childhood and adolescence. And Harold had been my closest friend since I was five years old. And the whole of my past life was to be wiped out for . . . Eleanor Farjeon!—a woman I had only met once or twice in my life.

I wrote back a mollifying letter to Lawrence asking him, indeed imploring him, not to endanger the reputations of Keynes, Duncan and Frankie. And for myself I decided that my friendship with Lawrence was over. I was greatly moved by the warm affection—no, love—shown in Frieda's letter.

Now, reading it sixty-three years after it was written, I am struck not only by the love and sympathy she showed in it but by her wisdom and her belief in me. Far less emotional than Lawrence, she saw things very much more clearly.

Lawrence was barking up the wrong tree. Although at first I returned Frankie's embraces, after a little while I was unable to do so. I was very fond of him, but physical contact became unpleasant. What had been a sentimental love on his part and a flattered readiness to experiment on mine, developed into a happy and hilarious friendship. While writing this, it has occurred to me that the best reply I could have made to Lawrence's letter would have been to have made love to Frieda. But the idea comes sixty-three years too late.

It is ironical that two years after Lawrence's diatribe he developed an intense friendship with a young Cornish farmer, which Frieda thought had a sexual element, as she told me after the war in 1923. And to Mabel Luhan's question, she replied: 'I think so. It made me dreadfully unhappy.'

But soon after his letter to me Lawrence was seen consorting with the black-beetles. Lytton Strachey wrote to me on 10 November 1915 describing seeing Lawrence for the first time at Brett's studio. The Hon. Dorothy Brett was a Slade student contemporary with Gertler, Carrington, Barbara Hiles and John Nash.

... a great many people I did not know at all and others whom I only knew by repute, among the latter Lawrences, whom I examined carefully and closely for several hours, though I didn't venture to have myself introduced. I was surprised to find that I liked her looks very much—she actually seemed (there's no other word for it) a lady: as for him I've rarely seen anyone so pathetic, miserable, ill, and obviously devoured by internal distresses. He behaved to everyone with the greatest cordiality, but I noticed for a second a look of intense disgust and hatred flash into his face ... caused by ... ah!—whom?

It is no good guessing who it was. Lytton's letter continued after the description of another party,

The principal news is that Lawrence's novel [*The Rainbow*] has been suppressed by the police. It seems strange that they should have the leisure and energy for that sort of activity at the present moment. But no doubt the authorities want to show us that England stands for Liberty. Clive is trying to get up an agitation about it in the newspapers, but I doubt if he'll have much success. We interviewed that little worm Jack Squire, who quite failed to see the point: he thought that as in his opinion the book wasn't a good one it was difficult for him to complain about its suppression. Damn his eyes! In vain we pointed out that it was a question of principle, and that whether that particular book was good or mediocre was irrelevant—he couldn't see it. At last, however, he agreed to say a few words about it in his blasted paper—on one condition—that the book had not been suppressed because it mentioned sapphism—he had heard that that was the reason—and in that case—well—it was quite impossible for the *New Statesman* to defend perversity.

Soon afterwards Lawrence and Frieda had lunch at 46 Gordon Square with Clive and Vanessa Bell and Jack and Mary Hutchinson to make plans for the best course of action. In a letter written at this time Duncan Grant wrote to me: 'A new book of Georgian verse has appeared with three poems by Lawrence in it. They are a surprise to me and very good and all attempting something like poetry.'

I was alone in Paris when I heard of the seizure of *The Rainbow*. I felt very angry and wrote an indignant letter to Frankie's father, Augustine Birrell, who was still a cabinet minister, invoking the shade of Milton. I got an unsympathetic reply. It was the loathsome black-beetles who rallied in defence of Lawrence.

I did not see him again until Armistice night, 11 November 1918. It was for the last time. I had gone to work that morning, but when the news came, Duncan and I downed tools, bicycled into Lewes and went to London. The city had gone mad. It was glorious. Bus-loads of munition workers, their gay faces stained yellow with T.N.T., explored the West End. The taxis carried loads of passengers on their roofs. Trafalgar Square was so densely packed with dancers that it was impassable.

That evening I went to a party in Montagu Shearman's flat in the Adelphi. It was crammed with my friends and acquaintances. Lytton Strachey and Carrington, Jack and Mary Hutchinson, Osbert Sitwell, Lawrence and Frieda. There were also Diaghilev and Massine, Henry Mond and his mother.

I had not seen Lawrence or Frieda for three years, and in a rush of pleasure went up to speak to him. Frieda gave me an affectionate squeeze on seeing me, but Lawrence only said, 'So you're here,' and went on talking. He looked ill and unhappy, with no trace of that gay sparkling love of life in his eyes, which had been his most attractive feature six years before.

Later on he was ready to talk to me, and several people crowded round to listen. I cannot reproduce his actual words, but the gist of what he said was this:

'I suppose you think the war is over, and that we shall go back to the kind of world you lived in before. But the war isn't over. The hate and evil are greater now than ever. Very soon war will break out again and overwhelm you. It makes me sick to see you rejoicing like a butterfly in the last rays of the sun before the winter. The crowd outside thinks that Germany is crushed forever. But the Germans will soon rise again, and Europe is done for. England most of all the countries. The war isn't over. Even if the fighting should stop, the evil will be worse, because the hate will be dammed up in men's hearts and will show itself in all sorts of ways which will be worse than war. Whatever happens there can be no peace on earth.'

There was a sombre joy in which he made these prophecies, and I could see that he was enjoying being the only man in the room who was not rejoicing because men were no longer killing each other. The impression he made on me was so antipathetic that I did not try and seek him out during the year he remained in England. And on the rare occasions that he came back I did not see him either, though Frieda came to see me.

I did not read *Whistling of Birds* until years later. But what he wrote then shows that he felt what we were all feeling that night of joy—but that it took some months for the message to reach him.

The man who declared there could be no peace but only more hate and evil, wrote:

> We follow with our eyes the bloody and horrid march of extreme winter, as it passes away. But we cannot hold back the spring. . . Whether we will or no, the daphne tree will soon be giving off perfume, the lambs dancing on two feet, the celandines will twinkle all over the ground, there will be a new heaven and a new earth . . . we have no choice, the spring is within us, the silver fountain begins to bubble under our breast, there is gladness in spite of ourselves. And on the instant we accept the gladness! The first day of change, out whistles an unusual, uninterrupted pæan, a fragment that will augment itself imperceptibly. And this in spite of the extreme bitterness of the suffering, in spite of myriads of torn dead.

The prophet who saw nothing but hatred and evil, who felt sick at the sight of a butterfly fluttering in the last rays of the sun, was also the great writer and poet who later on could express our emotion better than any of us dancing on that night.

Edward Morgan Forster

Edward Morgan Forster

'We did not see much of Forster at that time, who was already the elusive colt of a dark horse,' Lord Keynes wrote of the years about 1902 when he was forming his early beliefs, based on the philosophy of G. E. Moore and the discussions in the Society, otherwise known as the Apostles. Leonard Woolf wrote of that period: 'Forster and Desmond MacCarthy moved erratically in and out of this solar system of intellectual friendship, like comets.'

The explanation of Morgan's making only occasional appearances was the difference in age, which is never more important than at school and the university. He was four years older than Maynard Keynes. He had gone down in 1901, two years before the publication of *Principia Ethica*, and on his visits to Cambridge, talk with Goldsworthy Lowes Dickinson and Nathaniel Wedd was more important to him than the discussions of his juniors. What was true of Cambridge was true of 'Bloomsbury', which was formed by the children of Sir Leslie Stephen unconsciously gathering around them a group of men whose friendships and beliefs had been formed at Cambridge at the same time.

Dickinson and Wedd were the most formative influences for Morgan as regards ethics, though he completely accepted Moore's doctrine that since it is impossible to calculate the final results of any act, one must only take into account the immediate results. Thus a barbarous or brutal action cannot be justified because its effects may be beneficial in the long run. Forster applied this not only to the bombing of a city, but to every form of unkindness. What was true of ethics was also true of art and literature. Morgan was an established writer ten years before the publication of Virginia Woolf's first novel, *The Voyage Out*, and thirteen before Lytton Strachey's *Eminent Victorians*. Morgan's closest friend in Bloomsbury was Leonard Woolf, absent in Ceylon while Morgan was writing his early novels. But it was owing to Leonard that he completed *A Passage to India*, which he had abandoned in despair.

E. M. FORSTER
painting by Carrington

Morgan did not take criticism well in his later years. He had been modest as a young man, but an author's vanity increases with the years, and Morgan came to regard himself as a very great writer. He resented the fact that not all the members of Bloomsbury could wholeheartedly agree.

It is difficult not to be critical of his work. Pan shows his cloven hoof in almost everything he wrote, and I always felt, and still feel, that Morgan had never actually met that god. Edward had told him that his symbolisations of sex were often out of key, and his Bloomsbury critics were ready to tell him that they were out of place altogether. Thus in so far as they did influence him, it was by restraining him from introducing Pan round the Corner. Morgan recalls that *The Point of It* 'was ill-liked when it came out by my Bloomsbury friends. "What *is* the point of it?" they queried thinly, nor did I know how to reply.'

He respected Leonard more than any of them and thought of him as a practical man from whom to seek advice when in difficulty. When, in the beginning of 1922, he was invited to go out to India as temporary Private Secretary to the Maharajah of Dewas, Senior, Morgan thought he ought to be able to ride a horse. Instead of going to a riding school, he consulted Leonard and asked him to give him lessons. Leonard agreed and taught him to ride in Richmond Park. But more remarkable was his asking Leonard to be present, in the next room, while he was having his tonsils removed. The operation took place in my mother-in-law's house, 27 Brunswick Square, where Morgan had a room, and while it was being performed Leonard and Mrs Marshall sat and talked. When Morgan came to from the anaesthetic, Leonard went in and told him that all was well and that he would soon be better, and then went home. Morgan shared the trust that so many people, particularly the young and simple, and all animals, felt for Leonard, but which, I confess, I did not feel myself.

It is possible that without the restraining influence of Leonard, the immanent spirit of the Marabar Caves might have become an overt presence disastrous to the credibility of *A Passage to India*, which I regard as the finest of his books, and which had great political influence.

But if Morgan sought Leonard's advice, Virginia came to respect and depend on his criticism and good opinion of her writing more than on that of Lytton Strachey, or Clive Bell, or Roger Fry. His importance to her is described in her diary written after a visit by Forster to Hogarth House and a walk along the bank of the Thames.

'We talked very rarely, the proof being that we (I anyhow) did not mind silences. Morgan has the artist's mind; he says the simple things that clever people don't say. I find him the best of critics for that reason. Suddenly out comes the obvious thing that one has overlooked.'

I first saw Morgan when I was a schoolboy and my father brought him back to tea to meet my mother. I had read one of his books and was surprised by his being so young.

I read each of them as it came out and liked *A Room With a View* best. I did not see him again until the first year of the war, when I met him at one of Lady Ottoline Morrell's parties. The next day, going to Duncan Grant's studio, I found Morgan there. Then the bell sounded and I ran down and admitted D. H. Lawrence and Frieda, who had been sent to look at Duncan's pictures by Lady Ottoline. After one or two of the pictures had been set up on the easel, Lawrence began a harangue and an expression of pain came into Morgan's face. Since then I have often seen him wince when a brutal or insensitive remark has been made. Usually it was only for a moment before he braced himself to face the harshness of the outside world. But as Lawrence launched himself upon the evil that he detected in Duncan's paintings, the look of pain was replaced by one of pure misery, and soon he murmured something about a train to Weybridge and disappeared.

Catching the train to Weybridge, where he lived with his mother, was an invaluable excuse for avoiding either boredom, or a distressing scene, and on that occasion Lawrence provided both, though it would have had a comic side for the thick-skinned. That, most certainly, none of us were—Morgan the least of all.

Though the wince of pain is one of my most vivid memories of Morgan, the delighted appreciation of a remark is a more frequent one. His broad, rather heart-shaped face would light up, the eyes would sparkle, and a sort of suppressed sneeze, which became a surreptitious laugh, would reveal how much he had been pleased and amused. It was a pleasure that was almost anguish. I have most often witnessed this reaction at meetings of the Memoir Club. Sometimes a preliminary look of pain would be followed by the little sneeze of joy when he listened to the inspired gossip of Bloomsbury—gossip which its chroniclers stigmatise as malicious, but which was actually the result of an almost gourmet-like love of the foibles of old and intimate friends. What would be malicious if told about a stranger or a slight acquaintance may be free of malice if told about a loved one. Such were the anecdotes about Vanessa and Duncan and Roger Fry. And rich and varied they were.

Morgan had lent Duncan the manuscript of a secret and unpublishable novel, called *Maurice*, a book which has been published after Morgan's death. When I read it first, illicitly, I thought it boring and could scarcely finish it. Even in 1915 it was out of date. I have just read it again. It is a propaganda novel about a congenital homosexual growing up to discover he is afflicted with an 'unspeakable vice' which he is unable to indulge, and the loneliness which results is the chief part of the book. Finally the under-keeper on his friend's estate climbs into his bedroom at night. The keeper later tries to blackmail him, but all ends happily with their going off together to become manual workers.

The faults of the book are that the early part is far too long and that the solution of Maurice's problem carries no conviction. It has therefore the faults of most propaganda. There are, as one might expect, good scenes, but the interest is in what it reveals about the author.

Morgan was responsible for getting my first story published. It was about a soldier's loneliness when he got home after the war, and I wrote it in 1919. Duncan sent a copy to Morgan who passed it on with a recommendation to the Editor of the *English Review*.

I did not meet him then, but two years later, after I had started a bookshop, he formed a habit of dropping in fairly often. I discovered that Arnold, his publisher, had several of his novels still in print in first editions, for in those happier days an author's books were not remaindered directly sales dropped off. Morgan could no doubt have obtained copies at trade price, but he preferred to encourage us and he gave away many copies of his books. He also used his influence to obtain two valuable customers for us: the education department of the Palestine Government, then under British Mandate, and that of the state of Hyderabad. Knowing that I was hard up, he also procured me the job of reviewing books for the *Daily Herald*.

After I gave up being a bookseller, Stephen Tomlin, Francis Birrell and I founded a little dining club, and we did not hesitate to invite all the distinguished men we knew to become members, and most of them accepted. Morgan was one and attended our meetings fairly regularly. On one occasion—it must have been in the summer when members were on holiday—Morgan and I were the only ones who turned up. We had a delightful dinner together, and I am glad to say the experience did not put him off attending afterwards.

After the death of 'Lawrence of Arabia', Morgan was asked to edit a volume of his letters. His plan—of dividing the book into sections, each dealing with one of T.E.'s different interests, was not approved by T.E.'s brother, Arnold Lawrence, who then asked me to edit the book. I also thought that Morgan's plan had been a bad one. He showed no sign of resentment, and he put all his notes at my disposal and helped me as much as he could.

In later years we saw each other at the Memoir Club with the élite of Bloomsbury.

The most delightful of our meetings was held one summer at Charleston in the garden. We lounged about. It was a pleasure to look at Morgan's face: so happy, so relaxed, so full of enjoyment as he listened to Vanessa reading.

A much later meeting of the Memoir Club was disastrous. We had our dinner at a restaurant in Sloane Square and adjourned, perhaps to Leonard's rooms in Victoria Square. Morgan read us some chapters of *Battersea Rise*. It soon became apparent that several of us were bored. We sat glumly, and Morgan's feelings were hurt. He never attended one of the Memoir Club meetings again.

There was nothing that could be done about it.

Morgan was one of the few members of the Reform Club whom I knew and sometimes I was lucky enough for him to come over and sit down beside me. We would talk a little, and if I could coax that little sneeze of amusement—while he turned his face away, for I think he felt laughter was private—I was delighted.

After he came to live in King's College Cambridge I invited him to one of my birthday parties at Hilton Hall and to my great pleasure he came. He brought with him a birthday present: a tiny toy budgerigar, one of a pair that he had brought back from India.

'I keep my one on my writing-table and I like to think of you having the other,' he said. The little green painted bird with a patch of red on the wings, with barred yellow legs, stands now over the beam of my fireplace. It was a characteristic gift. During his visit there was the same expression of happiness on his broad face as I had remarked at the Charleston meeting.

Not very long before Morgan's death I was asked to contribute an article on E. M. Forster in Bloomsbury to a volume brought out in his honour. So I wrote to him and he asked me to have lunch with him in his rooms in King's.

'What are we going to talk about?' was the question with which he greeted me.

'Leonard,' I replied.

So we talked about Leonard and Virginia, and then about Lytton. He told me that his friends in Bloomsbury had had very little influence on his writing—he had done most of his work before he had got to know them well—but that my father, Edward, had reviewed *Where Angels Fear to Tread*, had got to know him and had given him advice on all his subsequent novels, except *A Passage to India*, and that they had often had lunch together at that early period.

Morgan may have exaggerated Edward's influence, partly to gratify me and partly to reject that he was a part of Bloomsbury and influenced by its members. But I think that he meant what he said, at all events while he was saying it.

He told me also that he had been much interested and pleased by the article I had written comparing his work and Galsworthy's. I have reprinted the gist of it here because I think it helps one to understand the work of each man by putting him into relation with its time and its audience. The reader will, I hope, forgive a few repetitions.

Forster and Galsworthy
Compared

The first thing to note is that they are both propagandists: social reformers. This is true of all Morgan's novels and of all of Galsworthy's work which is any good.

They are dated propaganda, written at the beginning of the twentieth century. They were concerned with the tyranny of conventions, the subjection of women and the indifference or contempt of the British upper middle class for all people of different race or origin.

Both hated the spirit of their age. Propaganda is of little value without understanding of the enemy. Lacking that, it is mere prejudice. Both Morgan Forster and Galsworthy had an inside knowledge of what they were attacking, which is why they are so much more effective than the crude propaganda of Brecht in the *Threepenny Opera* or of Shaw in *The Doctor's Dilemma*. Both Brecht and Shaw raise a laugh among the ignorant. And the lack of understanding of what they are attacking makes their propaganda irritating. They are delivering knock-out blows where there is no opponent, and slander those who abolished the abuses they attack. The propagandist who writes from the inside is very different. For example, it is because Orwell was once a communist that *Animal Farm* is such a devastating parable.

Before comparing the work of Forster and Galsworthy, look at the men. Galsworthy: a large bald head, level steely blue eyes, firm compressed lips, always correctly dressed for town or country by a Savile Row tailor, a rimless eyeglass dangling from a thin black cord, or screwed firmly into his right eye. Galsworthy was a man who held himself very upright and was very upright. He had little humour but could be jolly. He was the reverse of subtle—though the two warring elements in his nature enabled him to see both sides of many questions. He had a natural dislike of anything equivocal. He loved dogs and would always prefer to idealise women rather than to understand them. He had great ability but was rather rigid, with good intentions. I feel sure that he was incapable of believing that many serious matters are best treated frivolously.

Forster: a curious flat top to his head and a long inquisitive nose. A little laugh when he took your point and then, holding his head on one side and giving one or two little nods like a bird pecking at grain, he would return to present his question mark again. His questions were sly. When you showed that you had noticed his slyness, he laughed, pleased, and it was a bond between you. He was always drawing sharp distinctions and drawing them in unexpected places. He had great humour but was rarely jolly, though he would have liked to be. He was extremely subtle and often equivocal. He had an uncanny knowledge of elderly women and no illusions about young ones. He had a very high opinion of his own work.

He was usually inconspicuously dressed in smooth grey or mustardy tweeds which never looked very new and he often wore a knitted pullover which was probably given him at Christmas some years before. He was an affectionate man delighted by childish things.

You can see that two men could scarcely be less alike, but both were doing their best work at the same time.

Galsworthy's first book published under his own name, *The Island Pharisees*, appeared in 1904. His last book was published in 1931, and he died in 1933. Forster's first novel published in his lifetime, *Where Angels Fear to Tread*, came out in 1905, his last novel, *A Passage To India* in 1924. While Forster's appeal remained for many years restricted to the intelligentsia, Galsworthy's work underwent a change. He became a best-selling author and a very successful playwright and won an immense reputation abroad as well as in England. He refused a knighthood, but accepted the O.M., and there was a service at Westminster Abbey on his death.

Forster accepted a C.H. and an O.M. A commemorative concert was held in King's College hall, but no religious service. He had been a fellow of the College for several years.

In Forster's first book, *Where Angels Fear to Tread* British complacency is represented by Mrs Herriton. She has successfully prevented her son's silly widow from marrying again in England—why should a young woman who has had one husband want another? But the silly woman escapes with a female friend to Italy, where she quite inexcusably falls in love with a beautiful young Italian, the son of a dentist, and marries him before her brother-in-law can arrive in time to stop the marriage. It turns out, as all sensible people would have expected, to be a most unhappy one. Gino, the Italian, has married her for her money; he is mercenary, tyrannical, unfaithful.

The silly woman dies in giving birth to a son and the episode appears to be closed. But to Mrs Herriton's fury, the female friend demands to know what is being done about the baby and, hearing that nothing is being done, declares that she will adopt it and bring it back. Mrs Herriton's pride forbids that the half-brother of her grand-daughter should be adopted by a neighbour, and sees that she must adopt the unwanted child herself. She sends out her clever son Philip and her intensely stupid daughter, to buy the child for the lowest sum possible. But the mercenary father refuses to part with his son; he loves the baby and is actually marrying a woman without a dowry in order to have someone to look after the boy. Philip accepts defeat gladly, but his stupid sister kidnaps the child, which is killed when the carriage in which she is driving to the station overturns.

In Galsworthy's first book, *The Island Pharisees*, a perfectly conventional young man from Eton and Oxford, who has just got engaged to a charming upper-class girl, meets an undesirable French adventurer in a railway carriage and, for no ascertainable reason, sees English upper-class society in which he has been brought up through the Frenchman's eyes. The rest of the novel is an indictment of the British upper class. Finally the hero's engagement is broken off because the girl realises that he is viewing her world through the eyes of the French adventurer. *The Island Pharisees* is inspired by hatred. Galsworthy was an angry young man when he wrote it. Why was he angry? The reason was not economic. Galsworthy was rich, or living on a generous allowance given him by his father, whose wealth he would inherit. He had been educated at Harrow and Oxford, he was one of the ruling class. Had he stood for Parliament, he would have been elected and would almost certainly have soon got into the Cabinet and would have made a scrupulously honest politician of the finest type. Why should he be angry? Why should he make a moral survey of his own class and find it detestable? The explanation of this book and of several of Galsworthy's subsequent books—in fact of all the good books he ever wrote—is that he had fallen irretrievably in love with his cousin's wife and she with him. Galsworthy believed that if he and Ada were to go and live together the scandal would break his father's heart, and he adored his father.

Ada therefore continued for some years to live with the man she intensely disliked—until he went off to the Boer War, after which she lived illicitly with Jack. Finally 'Old Jolyon' of *The Forsyte Saga* died, there was a divorce, and Jack and Ada got married.

If we compare *Where Angels Fear to Tread* with *The Island Pharisees* we see that each book turns on a disturbing foreigner showing up the inhumanity of the British upper class, which is always willing to sacrifice natural emotion to the maintenance of good form. *Where Angels Fear to Tread* is a good book—not a very good one, but as good today as the day when it was written. *The Island Pharisees* is a very bad one. The insular attitude which they attacked has been blown to smithereens, though even without two wars and the disintegration of the British Empire, I think that the Wright Brothers, Marconi and Lord Rutherford would have destroyed it.

Forster, like Galsworthy, was an angry young man. To find out why, we must turn to his next novel, *The Longest Journey*. Ricky was a day boy at Sawston School. Day boys were disliked and harried by the masters, who found it financially profitable to be housemasters in charge of boarders. After he has been to Cambridge, Ricky falls in love and marries a conventional girl who never has doubts about what is right and what is wrong. Ricky has to take a job as an assistant master in his old school where he finds himself forced to side with the illiberal, organising, efficient innovators, who had made his own school days so unhappy. Eventually, owing to the existence of an unsuspected half-brother, who is a child of nature, Ricky breaks free of his wife and the school, and is run over by a train while pushing his drunk half-brother to safety.

The Longest Journey is much the worst of Forster's novels (except for the posthumous *Maurice*) but it tells us a great deal about its author. He had been a day boy at Tonbridge School and the experience had marked him for life. We are told that the child is the father of the man, and there is no doubt that the harried, over-organised and insulted day-boy at Tonbridge was the father of the Chairman of the Council for Civil Liberties, E. M. Forster. His treatment at school influenced his whole life, and *The Longest Journey* is an indictment not only of the complacent and vulgar materialism of the British middle classes, but also of the particularly unpleasant ways in which this quality manifests itself in schoolmasters.

Forster and Galsworthy are not only alike in attacking the society from which they sprang; their method of attack is curiously the same—

by the introduction of someone from outside the social class who shows up the falsity, hypocrisy and dishonesty of those inside it. In *Where Angels Fear to Tread* it is the Italian, Gino; in *The Longest Journey* it is Ricky's half-brother, the child of nature; and in each of his novels, except *A Passage to India*, the same symbolic figure occurs. But I never think this natural man of Forster's is very convincing.

We find Galsworthy using exactly the same method. The outside figure is not always a foreigner, or a member of another class. He may be an old man who has eccentric views. Thus in *A Room with a View* Forster has old Mr Emerson, of whom the clergyman says: 'He has the merit—if it is one—of saying exactly what he means. It is so difficult—at least I find it difficult—to understand people who speak the truth.' Mr Emerson is the touchstone who shows up the values of the conventional middle classes as genteel nonsense and brings the book to a happy ending by telling the heroine that, 'Love is of the body'—which she doesn't understand at once, but which makes her see that the engagement she had accepted would not do. In *Fraternity* Galsworthy has old Mr Stone, who plays a parallel role by reading aloud his endless book on *The Brotherhood of Man*. Of course Galsworthy would have found it distasteful to commit himself either directly, or through the mouth of Mr Stone, to such a statement as 'Love is of the body'.

Nevertheless their message is often very much the same. In *A Passage to India* Dr Aziz says:

No one can ever realize the kindness we Indians need, we do not even realize it ourselves. But we know when it has been given. Kindness, more kindness and even after that more kindness. It is the only hope.

It is kindness which the English consciously repudiate and refuse. 'We're not out here for the purpose of behaving pleasantly,' says Mrs Moore's son.

In *Fraternity*, Galsworthy elaborates the same theme as applied to the relations of English social reformers and the poor. Mr Stone explains that the proletariat is a heaving sea of creatures on which sails a fleet of cockle shells, in the stern of each of which is a social reformer, distending his cheeks and puffing at the sails:

Looking back on that pretty voyage we could see the reason why those ships were destined never to move. . . . The man who blew should have been in the sea, not on the ship.

It was mysterious unconscious love which was lacking to the windy efforts of those who tried to sail that fleet. They were full of reason, conscience, horror, full of impatience, contempt, revolt. But they did not love the masses of their fellow men. They could not fling themselves into the sea.

The message there is the same. But how different in other respects! The subject of *Fraternity* is what two Kensington upper-middle-class families are to do about their 'shadows' in the adjoining back streets, of whom they have become aware owing to Mrs Dallison needing a model for her picture. Originally she wanted a half-draped figure. 'But Bianca decided that after all the shadow was better represented fully clothed; for though she discussed the nude and looked upon it with freedom, when it came to painting unclothed people she felt a sort of physical aversion.'

The Dallisons feel responsible for the Little Model, and a great deal of their efforts on her behalf are directed to prevent her from getting work as a model—since this is bound to end in her having to sit naked. Galsworthy is in entire sympathy with their attitude; he does not poke fun at it. It seems self-evident to him. Yet it is the exact opposite of what any of us would do today.

In *The Man of Property*, Galsworthy wrote very frankly of Ada's situation. She is Irene, the wife of Soames Forsyte, Galsworthy's cousin. Soames engages an architect to build him a house in the country. This man, Bosinney, who is called the Buccaneer by the Forsytes, falls in love with Irene and she with him.

My father Edward Garnett was, I think, the first Englishman who did not care a damn for the Victorian social conventions and very little about money, or success, whom Galsworthy had got to know well, and Bosinney is closely modelled on my father. This led to an amusing situation. In the first version of *The Man of Property* Bosinney committed suicide because Soames had ruined him financially. Edward, without recognising himself, declared that Galsworthy did not understand a man of Bosinney's type, and that it was incredible that he should commit suicide about money. All that mattered to him was that Irene loved him. Galsworthy defended his interpretation, but my father, on stronger ground than he knew, stood firm and eventually forced Galsworthy to change the ending and have Bosinney run over in a fog. Galsworthy told the whole story in their published correspondence. Nevertheless the character of Bosinney is the weakest part of what, I think, is Galsworthy's best book.

There is however a good deal to be said for *The Country House*. At the beginning Galsworthy is still an angry man and critical of his own class,

'A LETTER TO JACK'
Edward Garnett writing to Galsworthy about Bosinney
watercolour sketch by E. M. Heath

as shown in the following passage, which I quote partly in order to show how well he can write:

What indeed could be more delightful than this country house life of Mr Pendyce's; its perfect cleanliness, its busy leisure, its combination of fresh air and scented warmth, its complete intellectual repose, its essential and professional aloofness from suffering of any kind and its soup—emblematically and above all its soup—made from the rich remains of pampered beasts?

Mr Pendyce thought his life the one right life; those who lived it the only right people. He considered it a duty to live this life, with its simple healthy yet luxurious curriculum, surrounded by creatures bred for his devouring, surrounded, as it were, by a sea of soup. And that people should go on existing by the million in towns, preying on each other and getting continually out of work, with all those other concomitants of an awkward state, distressed him. While surburban life, that living in little rows of slate-roofed houses so lamentably similar that no man of individual taste could bear to see them, he much disliked. Yet in spite of his strong prejudice in favour of the country house life, he was not a rich man, his income barely exceeding ten thousand a year.

In that passage there is affection mingling with the anger and the irony. But a change creeps into *The Country House* as the story unfolds. Galsworthy falls in love with his own class in the person of Mrs Pendyce. His love for her is sentimental. He loves her because she is his ideal of an aristocrat and a lady.

The subject of *The Country House* is that the world of Mr Pendyce is suddenly menaced by the scandal of a divorce in which his eldest son George would be the co-respondent. All ends well, as Mrs Pendyce visits the husband to tell him that his wife is no longer in love with her son. He kisses her hand and agrees to stop proceedings, saying: 'You're the only lady I know.'

I think that from that time on Galsworthy was really finished as a writer. His father died. Ada was divorced and married Jack. He devoted himself to literature and great causes. He remained upright and grew even more noble: his hatred of injustice and cruelty took many forms, but the bitterness which had started him writing evaporated. He became more and more benevolent, unconsciously falsifying and sentimentalising and inventing problems which had no real existence, in a series of trashy novels. His writing degenerated. He is frequently pretty awful in describing women. This is from *The Patrician*:

Wrapped in her new pale languor, still breathing deeply from the waltz, she seemed to Courtier too utterly moulded out of loveliness. To what end should a man frame speeches to a vision! She was but an incarnation of beauty imprinted on the air and would fade out at a touch—like the sudden ghosts of enchantment that came to one under the blue and the starlit snow of a mountain night, or in a birchwood and wistful, golden. Speech seemed but a desecration.

Not only is this foully written, but it is psychologically poppycock. If Courtier had been sixteen he might have felt something of the sort about a woman of thirty. But he is drawn from the adventurous figure of the great war correspondent, H. W. Nevinson. He is a man in his forties, who has been, we are told, the lover of many women, and it is quite incredible that he should have been dreaming about wistful birch trees and not watching what she was feeling. I knew Nevinson well, and it is impossible to imagine him ignoring reality for visions, or confusing the woman who attracted him with a ghost of enchantment.

While Galsworthy's characters became more unreal and his critical faculty increasingly blurred, Forster, perhaps because he published so little, showed a steady improvement and development. *Howards End* is a most excellent novel, but it cannot compare with *A Passage to India*. The plan of that book is on a grand scale: the friendship of an Englishman and a Mohammedan Indian through the crisis of a false accusation of sexual assault which brings out the worst in both races and the best qualities in one or two of them.

The characters are all individuals and freshly observed. But it is Forster's own interpolations and asides which are the great beauty and strength of the book. One is aware of his gentle, tender understanding of human failure:

And unlocking a drawer, he took out his wife's photograph. He gazed at it and tears spouted from his eyes. He thought, 'How unhappy I am!' But because he really was unhappy, another emotion soon mingled with his self-pity: he desired to remember his wife and could not. Why could he remember people whom he did not love? They were always so vivid to him, whereas the more he looked at this photograph the less he saw. She had eluded him thus, ever since they had carried her to her tomb. He had known that she would pass from his hands and eyes, but had thought she could live in his mind, not realizing that the very fact that we have loved the dead increases their unreality, and that the more passionately we invoke them the further they recede. A piece of brown cardboard and three children—that was all that was left of his wife. It was unbearable and he thought again: 'How unhappy I am!' and became happier.

That passage seems to me to be as true and as tender an observation as anything in any of the greatest novelists. Tolstoy might have made it.

It is interesting to compare the effect of Galsworthy's writings and of Forster's on events: to measure them against one another as propagandists. Galsworthy had a profound influence on all sorts of humanitarian causes. No doubt his greatest influence was on English prisons. He wrote *Justice*. The Home Secretary went to see it. As a result the maximum period for which prisoners could be kept in solitary confinement was reduced from nine to three months.

Forster, I think, influenced events with *A Passage to India* more than any author has influenced events with a novel in this century. It was read widely and fiercely resented, but nevertheless, its influence seeped in and then, acting like a hard frost, it began to break up the mortar in men's minds. It changed the climate. *A Passage to India* qualifies Forster to rank as the most effective propagandist novelist in English in this century. Galsworthy however is one of the runners-up. The eclipse of Galsworthy as a novelist was not permanent. There was a revival, due to television, like the revival of Trollope in the thirties. The public likes bad novels linked together by characters who appear in one after another. The Forsytes have acquired a period charm. An eclipse of Morgan has already occurred, but a revival will come in due course.

Virginia Woolf

Virginia Woolf

Virginia Woolf's father, Leslie Stephen, came of a family famous already in law and politics: particularly famous for the part its members played in the agitation against the slave trade. He added lustre to the family record, resigning a fellowship at Cambridge University because he was not prepared to take Holy Orders as a clergyman—which was then expected—as he realised that he was an agnostic (he himself coined the word), that is, he held an open mind with suspended belief on religious matters. On leaving the university he devoted himself to criticism and to literature. His first marriage, to Thackeray's daughter, was unhappy. She suffered from recurring fits of insanity.

After her death he married one of the most beautiful women in England, Mrs Julia Duckworth, who had been left a widow with two sons and one daughter. By her he had two sons and two daughters. They grew up in a large house in London, spending their holidays in Cornwall, surrounded by famous men and women, the friends of their parents. James Russell Lowell—then American Ambassador—was, as his letters show, not only a close friend and admirer of Leslie Stephen but for many years, until his death, the devoted friend of Julia. Henry James was a frequent visitor to the Stephen houses in London and in Cornwall. George Meredith was an equally close friend. The painter Watts, who had known Julia from a young girl, was a friend who painted their portraits; that of Leslie Stephen is good. That of Julia gives less idea of her beauty than the photographs taken by the pioneer photographer, her aunt, Mrs Cameron. But besides this background of culture and high thinking, there was a worldly element brought in partly by the Duckworth boys, partly by Stephen's eminence and Julia's beauty.

Mrs Cornish, who was famous for her directness, once came into a room where all the men were grouped round Julia Stephen and paying little attention to anyone else. Mrs Cornish looked at Julia, nodded her head and remarked, 'What a killjoy!'

VIRGINIA WOOLF
bust by Stephen Tomlin

GREAT FRIENDS

The background of the Stephen household is resurrected by Virginia in her novel, *To the Lighthouse*. But Julia died when Virginia was fourteen, and she grew up in the shadow of her eminent, querulous father, reading every book she could lay hands on, and trying to learn Greek by herself.

The Duckworth boys, grown up into smart worldly young men, did their utmost to bring their half-sisters out into society, and to arrange good marriages for them. Defeated by Vanessa after terrible scenes, George Duckworth turned to his younger sister. If Duncan Grant is to be believed, Virginia, in spite of her beauty, must have been unpromising material. Duncan wrote: 'Upon an unforeseen introduction for instance, there was an expression of blazing defiance, a few carefully chosen banalities, and a feeling of awkwardness.'

But even after the most ludicrous social disasters, George would slip into her bedroom, clasp Virginia in his arms and whisper 'Beloved'. The poor fellow not only felt it his sacred duty to marry his sisters to titled husbands, but was in love with them himself. It was natural enough: they were outstandingly beautiful, and he seemed incapable of realising their dislike of his embraces, as well as for all he stood for.

What follows is an escape story. But without Vanessa to organise their escape, and their brother Thoby to introduce Leonard Woolf and his friends from Cambridge, George Duckworth might have driven Virginia into an asylum for the whole of her life. As it was he did harm enough.

It was possible to escape from a half-brother: it might not have been from parents. If they had not lost both their parents early in life, the greatest English woman painter and the greatest woman writer of the first half of the twentieth century would have probably made 'good' marriages, and their work would have been that of amateurs. Mrs Cornish called their mother a 'killjoy' perhaps not only because her beauty attracted all the men, but because she was gloomy, serious, devoted to good works, and was, except for her agnosticism, a conventional Victorian lady. If she had lived, Vanessa would have wasted hours in soup-kitchens which were better spent at her easel, and Virginia, married to some handsome young peer, would have ruined his life and done little else.

After Leslie Stephen's death Vanessa organised their escape, and they took a house, 46 Gordon Square, which they shared with their real brothers, Thoby and the youngest, Adrian. Then, after Thoby's death, Vanessa married his great friend, Clive Bell, and Virginia and Adrian went to live in Fitzroy Square. The spare rooms in both houses were often occupied by Thoby's friends from Cambridge; Bloomsbury had begun.

Shortly after their escape, Virginia burned her boats by taking part in the famous *Dreadnought* hoax got up by her brother Adrian. Anyone, or any institution that was pompous or took itself seriously, appealed to his sense of humour. 'The Establishment', to use a modernism, was fair game. Virginia in a burst of defiance took a leading part in the brilliantly successful practical joke. A telegram purporting to be from the Foreign Office was sent to the Admiral on board the *Dreadnought*, then the largest battleship in the world, saying that the Crown Prince of Abyssinia was coming down to look over the *Dreadnought*, and the Admiral was asked to show him every courtesy. Virginia was disguised as the Crown Prince, Adrian a supposed interpreter, Duncan Grant a member of the Prince's suite, Horace Cole an official from the Foreign Office.

The practical joke caused a furore. It was a mere escapade and flouting of authority, but it was the kind of escapade that Victorian dowagers were not willing to condone.

The liberation they had sought was complete, and it went a long way. One day, when Virginia and Vanessa were alone, 'the door opened and the long and sinister figure of Mr Lytton Strachey stood on the threshold. He pointed his finger at a stain on Vanessa's white dress. "Semen?" he asked. Can one really say it? I thought & we burst out laughing. With that one word all our barriers of reticence and reserve went down.'

That quotation from a paper Virginia read to the Memoir Club shows that the Stephen sisters were unusual young women.

The so-called Bloomsbury circle, of which its members were never conscious, owed its existence to them. They had inherited all of their mother's beauty and their father's clear-minded intelligence. No man, however intelligent or free-spoken, had to adapt his lightest conversation, or most serious discussions in an argument, to their presence. They were fully the equals in wit and in wisdom and originality of mind of the men around them: Lytton Strachey, Clive Bell, Desmond MacCarthy, Morgan Forster and Leonard Woolf.

The latter had been a close friend at Cambridge of Lytton Strachey, and had then spent seven years as a British administrator in Ceylon. He had won golden opinions from his superiors, and there is little doubt that he had been marked out as a future Governor of Ceylon. But during his leave he fell passionately in love with Virginia and resigned his job in the hope that she would marry him. Two years before the 1914–18 War, she finally did.

Although they were devoted to each other, and Virginia was indeed in many ways dependent on Leonard's moral support, the marriage was clouded by Virginia's recurrent fits of insanity. These were connected with her writing, and were liable to come on after the strain of finishing one of her novels. During one of these lapses she heard the birds in the trees singing in Greek; sometimes she was violent. Leonard was forever on the watch and by keeping her from overworking, or going to too many parties—which she loved—he was able to ward off these attacks. I never saw any traces of madness in her, but I think her genius owed much to her nervous instability, and that her wildly poetical imagination was often only just this side of the borderline.

I first saw Virginia while she was still the fierce creature that Duncan describes. It was at a fancy-dress ball in aid of Women's Suffrage at Crosby Hall very soon after it had been re-erected in Cheyne Walk. Wagner was the greatest of musicians then, and all the cultured who could afford it went to hear *The Ring* at Bayreuth. So Virginia was dressed as a Valkyrie. She was very slim and astonishingly beautiful as she stood at gaze near me and Adrian, who was already a friend of mine.

Then she caught sight of a female friend on the other side of the ballroom and swooped on her like a falcon.

She was then at work on her first novel, *The Voyage Out*, which was accepted for publication by her half-brother Gerald Duckworth. She married Leonard Woolf in August 1912. Her health went up and down. Then a year later she had to enter a nursing home. It was partly to give Virginia an unexciting occupation, partly in order to print and publish, that Leonard bought a printing press so that she could set up her own stories. Such experimental writings would not have found a publisher in the first war. Thus the Hogarth Press came into existence, named after their house in Richmond. It was not until 1924 that they moved to 52 Tavistock Square, just round the corner from where their closest friends and relatives were living. Her niece, Angelica, wrote this description of Virginia there:

She was the most enchanting aunt that anyone is ever likely to have. . . To start with there was her beauty, her rare and special physical beauty which reminded one of the most aristocratic and nervous of racehorses or greyhounds and which fascinated me and possessed me even as a child. Her face with its vulnerable narrow temples and deeply hooded grey-green eyes shutting at an unexpected moment like the eyes of a bird and then opening to pierce me with a glance of amused intelligence. Above all her sensitive and sardonic mouth with a very pronounced downward curve, expressive often of the most intense amusement. Then her gestures which were somewhat jerky, her long hands waving a still longer cigarette-holder. She would puff the smoke out of the corner of her mouth and chuckle at some secret and intimate joke that we shared between us.

I remember going round to have tea with her at No. 52 Tavistock Square. I would climb the rather bleak stone stairs and be let in by the maid half-way up, and when at last at the top, Virginia would be there to welcome me, longlegged, long-fingered, and with silver hair escaping about her head. . . .

Leonard would come up from the cellar in which was the office of the Hogarth Press and have tea with us . . . and Virginia would call him Leo, almost as though she were trying to make me think of him as a noble lion with a mane and then she would banter him through me. 'What shall we make old Leo tell us about?' she would say. 'Has he caught many mice today in the cellar?' Leonard would take very little notice of this sort of affectionate and whimsical baiting. He would turn and look at me with the bluest of blue eyes fringed with the blackest of lashes and start on some different subject. It made me feel like an eaglet in its nest sitting between those two pairs of eyes, so different in quality—Leonard's the most intense of the two, Virginia's opening with surprise or gleaming with amusement, but each pair fastened on me with genuine and flattering interest in all my minute and childish affairs and friendships and the occurrences of daily life.

When Virginia's nephew, Julian Bell, was at Cambridge he gave a picnic at Quy Fen at which she was present. My sons Richard and William were about seven and five years old, and they must have heard that 'the Woolves are coming'. After we had bathed and had our lunch, I saw the little boys scrambling away among some willow bushes and then returning to bait Virginia, who was pursuing them on all fours, growling that she was a she-wolf. I think the game may have been all the more thrilling because tinged with a touch of fear. There was just the faintest possibility that she might not be like the foster-mother of Romulus and Remus, but an actual werewolf. Her growls were convincing.

Angelica also gives a description of visiting Virginia at Monk's House, Rodmell, not far from her own home Charleston, in Sussex.

. . . it was in the country that she seemed her happiest. Going over to tea with her at Rodmell was a constant pleasure to us during the summer holidays. Virginia would preside over the teapot in the dining-room, which was on a lower level than the garden outside. The green light filtering down through the leaves of plants pressed against the window panes intensified the feeling that she was the Queen of a translucent underwater world. But it was a world full of fun and gaiety and sparkling warmth. A great deal of teasing would go on and bursts of laughter as Virginia's flights of fancy became more and more unpredictable. After tea we swam out into the open and had a game of bowls, which we played on the Woolfs' lawn overlooked by the village church and ourselves overlooking the Ouse valley, which stretched away into the distance until it was met and bounded by Mount Caburn.

I almost always saw Leonard and Virginia together. During the war they would arrive on bicycles, Virginia a bit flushed, her eyes sparkling as she took in the faces of the company, Leonard silent, lean and mossy, greeting me very quietly, or speaking only to his spaniel to curb its demonstrations. Virginia's went uncurbed.

When I went to their house, it was Leonard who would open the door, and after his quiet greeting, I would go in and find Virginia still somewhat tempestuous and storm-tossed even indoors. She was a sea that I never saw in a flat calm: the wind was always blowing, the waves breaking. Her mind had the same sweeping quality.

I never knew what Virginia would talk about or what she would say, but I did know what she would not. She would never make the living into the dead, or the concrete into the abstract. She would never try to harmonise or streamline her hearers' conflicting ideas and sense-impressions into a uniform, consistent, neutral-tinted world. She would not generalise, she would always particularise; never flatten the focus, always heighten the three-dimensional depth of detail. Her imagination ranged in a world in which everything was alive. She knew that every living thing is unique, that only when its unique quality is perceived can it be understood and can become a subject for art.

It was the unlikenesses that she looked for not the likenesses. When the revelation of some unique quality in the person she was talking about, or talking to, came to her, she would stretch her neck out like a bird and crow with delighted laughter, and her voice in moments of excitement would break and split like an adolescent schoolboy's.

She was interested in everyone. She responded to young men and girls who aspired to write; she entered the make-believe worlds of children; she was fascinated by the old familiar figures of her childhood; the friends and relatives of her father's and of her girlhood, some shrivelled by time, some still brightly vigorous, some horribly decaying. She could be wittily sharp and cruel about those she disliked.

There was a strange contradiction in Virginia. She was so beautiful, so tall, so aristocratic and in many ways so fastidious. But she had a sense of humour that would stick at nothing, like Shakespeare's, or Chaucer's. And she had an appetite and a relish for life that one finds most often in market women.

Nothing made her wish to avert her eyes and cross to the other side of the street. Like Rembrandt she could have found the subject for a work of art in a side of beef.

Because of this there were no doors closed to her: she could pluck the secret from the heart of an old dried-up lawyer, a charwoman or a young actor enjoying his first triumph. Whenever Virginia appeared she brought a new treasure trove with her, something that she had heard in the street, been told over the counter, found in an old letter. After she had been to a party she would come round and regale her sister with an account of it, and what she said might have been written by Thackeray if he had been a poet with a completely uninhibited sense of humour. She was vain and sensitive to criticism, but she liked making herself into a ridiculous figure and laughing at herself.

Almost all her stories had one point, one object: to catch the unique living self that makes one human being different from another.

When she went into the street, she saw the same crowds that we all do, hurrying and scurrying along like disordered sheep. But for her the spectacle was, I think, an illusion. She never forgot that each figure was not a unit in a mass, but an individual with a secret. So that even in Oxford Street there was no crowd, and on the Downs the sheep were not a flock: the shepherd or his dog could tell each one apart.

To that I would add that as a young man I was well aware of her avidity to find out my secret feelings and of the ruthlessness with which she might use her knowledge, so for several years I was shy of her. If Mr Albee had been born to ask his question, 'Who's afraid of Virginia Woolf?' I should have admitted that I was.

But as time went on I felt more sure of her. She used to call me her badger—not Bunny, as other people did—and from the way in which she asked, 'How's my old Badger? What's he been writing?' I knew that she felt an amused but warm affection for me. Then, in the year before her death, when she realised that Angelica was in love with me, her love embraced us both, and she was a most comforting support, whatever her doubts about Angelica's wisdom.

I cannot improve upon my wife's description of Virginia's physical appearance, but I would add this: that she was beautiful with a beauty that gave the lie to Shakespeare's lament in the sonnet:

GREAT FRIENDS

When forty winters shall besiege thy brow
And dig deep trenches in thy beauty's field,
Thy youth's proud livery, so gazed on now,
Will be a tattered weed, of small worth held.

Virginia was fifty-nine at the time of her death, but the signs of that siege, the presence of those trenches, did not subtract from her beauty. The hollow temples, hollow hooded eyes, and almost fleshless face were as lovely as the beauty she had as a girl in her twenties when I first remember her.

Virginia committed suicide. The war horrified her, and the sky in Sussex was often full of fighting aircraft. She felt madness coming on and found death in the river. Angelica and I had seen her two days before, and she had never been warmer, or expressed her love for us more freely.

Dogmatising about the sexes is foolish. I only hazard a suggestion here because it may explain a quality in Virginia Woolf's work. For she made what men regard as a weakness in women's minds, her strength. Her originality as a writer was largely in expressing it. Women, it is said, do not concentrate. They can attend to the subject in hand, but their attention has not the wholeheartedness of a man's. If so, it is just possible that since women have been cooking the supper, mending clothes, listening to half-a-dozen children all talking at once, and keeping them good-tempered and amused since before the dawn of history, they have learned to be able to attend to several things at a time. A man, on the other hand, focuses his mind. A watch has stopped, let us say. Time and space and his environment cease to exist for him when he begins taking it to pieces and analysing the possible reasons for it going wrong.

In art and literature men do the same. They concentrate on one point after another, and the result is a series of events or facts or statements, logically related together, on which the mind is focused, as our eyes are focused on the illuminated patch of road when we drive at night. We do not see what is in the woods or fields on either side of the road. Almost all women writers have imitated men more or less successfully in this. But Virginia Woolf's work resembles that of the woman who is mending clothes in the kitchen while she watches pots simmering on the stove and tells a story to the children around her knee without forgetting that there is a home-made cake in the oven which, judging from the smell, will soon be ready to come out.

VIRGINIA WOOLF AND ETHEL SMYTH

In other words, time, space and the environment never cease to exist for Virginia. One of her chief interests, or at any rate one of the things she is always aware of, is relative motion.

But there was no silence; all the time the motor omnibuses were turning their wheels and changing their gear; like a vast nest of Chinese boxes all of wrought steel turning ceaselessly one within another the city murmured; on the top of which the voices cried aloud, and the petals of myriads of flowers flashed their colours into the air.

That last sentence of the little sketch *Kew Gardens*, written towards the end of the First World War, illustrates a preoccupation of Virginia's mind. All her subsequent novels and stories show the same absorbed interest in, and awareness of, simultaneous motions which are independent of each other. It was by the means of that awareness that she developed her very individual method of telling her stories and exhibiting her characters to the reader.

Jacob in *Jacob's Room* is shown to us as a young man through the eyes of old Mrs Norman protesting feebly as he enters the railway compartment, 'This is not a smoking-carriage' and imagining that she would throw her scent bottle with her right hand, and tug the communication cord with her left, if he assaulted her. 'She was fifty years of age, and had a son at college. Nevertheless it is a fact that men are dangerous.' She sees his face and is reassured. We see Jacob through her eyes as he travels to Cambridge, then as she gets out: 'this sight of her fellow-traveller was completely lost in her mind, as the crooked pin dropped by a child into the wishing-well twirls in the water and disappears forever.'

That image is an illustration of Virginia Woolf's other most remarkable quality as a writer. The prose is like poetry. The language is as sensitive to the beauty of things as the writer is to the multiplicity of events. The dispersion of attention that might have become a trick is never so in her. It is never a formula, but the expression of her individual taste and as carefully chosen, as inevitable, as her taste in words. In Bloomsbury we were all living very much in a world of painters, looking at pictures all the time, and listening to discussions which were always devoted to the visual arts rather than to literature. Indeed for many years I was accustomed to hear the adjective 'literary' used only as a term of abuse. I think Virginia learned something about her art from the painters and art critics, from watching her sister Vanessa and Duncan Grant paint, from listening to Roger Fry and Clive Bell. The latter greatly encouraged her when she was writing her first novel.

Some critics have been rash enough to say that Virginia Woolf drew not only the theme of *Mrs Dalloway* from James Joyce's *Ulysses* but her literary method as well. I don't believe they know what the theme of *Mrs Dalloway* is. And as for literary method! *Mrs Dalloway* derives directly from *Jacob's Room* in method. And the origin of *Jacob's Room* was, as we know from Virginia's diary, her experiments in writing, *The Mark on the Wall* and *Kew Gardens* which, she said, shake hands and dance.

The Mark on the Wall was published in 1917, and *Kew Gardens* set up in type and published in 1919—the year in which she read the first excerpts from *Ulysses* in the *Little Review*.

Not that there are no literary influences. If, as Angelica suggested, she Virginia were a racehorse, I should expect to find Laurence Sterne and Henry James in her pedigree. The opening chapters of *Night and Day* have a distinct flavour of James. Later on, though the texture of her writing is quite unlike that of Henry James, there is the same kind of sensitive analysis characteristic of the novels of James's middle period.

VIRGINIA WOOLF

On her writing-table at Asheham she kept a framed and autographed photograph of Henry James. And surely anyone can see in the wilful interruption of the narrative, which turns out to be so relevant to the matter in hand, an echo of *Tristram Shandy*?

The theme of *Mrs Dalloway* is probably more easily missed by the younger generation and by foreigners than by those who grew up surrounded by the English social scene before the first war. The theme of *Mrs Dalloway* is the death of the soul, or perhaps one should say the withering, for death is an exaggeration. It is the study of a woman who as a girl had her chance but took the wrong turning, who failed to realise her highest potentialities by timidly sticking to the traditions of her class.

Peter Walsh, who had been in love with her, puts it clearly:

> There was always something cold in Clarissa, he thought. She had always, even as a girl, a sort of timidity, which in middle age becomes conventionality, and then it's all up, it's all up, he thought, looking rather drearily into the glassy depths, and wondering whether by calling at that hour he had annoyed her. . .

And it is Peter Walsh, who waking suddenly after dozing in the park, puts a name to it by exclaiming: 'the death of the soul'. Now whatever the theme of Joyce's *Ulysses* may be, it certainly is not the death of the soul resulting from too rigid an adherence to the conventions and too great a love of social success and of respectability. Clarissa Dalloway took the wrong turning when she was a girl. Her gay, irresponsible friend Sally, and Peter Walsh, who awakened her mind, but whom she rejected, represent the intellectual who values personal freedom and spontaneity and truth above social and monetary success—that is to say—Virginia Woolf's world, which she, and her sister Vanessa Stephen, very definitely chose, in opposition to the world of her half-brothers, the Duckworths. Peter Walsh indeed has the independence of mind of Leonard Woolf, although Peter is not as intelligent as Leonard, nor is he a Jew. And the novel, which is an account of a day in the life of Mrs Dalloway, is an analysis of just how and why she had failed to live up to the hopes of two most intimate friends, who had chosen freedom. It was partly cowardice in her, but perhaps also a certain idealistic loyalty to the traditions of her class. This is shown by her admiration for Lady Bexborough who had been billed to open some charity, and who carried out her engagement while she held in her hand the telegram which had that moment reached her, announcing her son's death in battle. *Noblesse oblige*. One may be appalled and horrified by some examples of the tradition of *noblesse oblige*. One may regard it as inhuman, but one respects it. And *noblesse oblige* is deep, deep in what are still the British upper classes. Politically it is something of immense value: a fascist leader like General Franco, a civil war like that in Spain, have been unthinkable in England because the tradition of *noblesse oblige* forbids them.

The comic side, the contemptible side of Mrs Dalloway's world is represented by Hugh Whitbread who has a job at court 'blacking the King's boots', his friends say unkindly. But all the same in spite of his greediness, snobbishness, fatness and general imbecility, Virginia has a sneaking liking for him because he is a gentleman and invariably considerate of other people's feelings, although of course he doesn't know what they are.

Clarissa Dalloway goes out shopping, meets her friends, returns home a little embittered because her husband has been asked to lunch without her, although it was only to meet Hugh Whitbread, who is helping Lady Bruton to write a letter to *The Times*.

Peter Walsh has come back that day from India, just as Leonard Woolf had returned from Ceylon. He is invited to Clarissa Dalloway's party that evening, preparations for which have already disorganised her household.

Virginia gives a perfectly astonishing picture of the surface of London as it was in the early twenties. The spirit of the West End of fashionable London glittering during the season in June has never been brought so well between the covers of a book. The prose descriptions are full of poetry; no one else's prose is so full of poetry. Even the clouds sailing overhead are not forgotten:

A puff of wind (in spite of the heat, there was quite a wind) blew a thin black veil over the sun and over the Strand. The faces faded; the omnibuses suddenly lost their glow. For although the clouds were of mountainous white so that one could fancy hacking hard chips off with a hatchet, with broad golden slopes, lawns of celestial pleasure gardens, on their flanks, and had all the appearance of settled habitations assembled for the conference of the gods above the world, there was a perpetual movement among them. Signs were interchanged, when, as if to fulfil some scheme arranged already, now a summit dwindled, now a whole block of pyramidal size which had kept its station inalterably advanced into the midst or gravely led the procession to fresh anchorage. Fixed as they seemed at their posts, at rest in perfect unanimity, nothing could be fresher, freer, more sensitive superficially than the snow-white or gold-kindled surface; to change, to go, to dismantle the solemn assemblage was immediately possible; and in spite of the grave fixity, the accumulated robustness and solidity, now they struck light to the earth, now darkness.

And then she introduces what at first sight appears to be a complete irrelevance—the study of Septimus Smith and his Italian wife. Septimus has fought in the war and delayed shell-shock has resulted in madness. His delusions are drawn from personal experience:

> Men must not cut down trees. There is a God. (He noted such revelations on the backs of envelopes.) Change the world. No one kills from hatred. Make it known (he wrote it down). He waited. He listened. A sparrow perched on the railing opposite chirped Septimus, Septimus, four or five times over and went on, drawing its notes out, to sing freshly and piercingly in Greek words how there is no crime and, joined by another sparrow, they sang in voices prolonged and piercing in Greek words, from trees in the meadow of life beyond a river where the dead walk, how there is no death.
>
> There was his hand; there the dead. White things were assembling behind the railings opposite. But he dared not look. Evans was behind the railings!

She is drawing madness from the inside. But what is Septimus doing in the book? What relation has he to Mrs Dalloway? I think that he is the shadow that throws the brilliant colours into relief. He is the reminder of what is just round the corner for each of us: madness, tragedy, death. Septimus and his unhappy wife deepen the book and add greatly to it. They are not irrelevant, for they are always there among us. We are aware of their tragedy during all the preparations for the party, and when Septimus throws himself out of a window to his death we meet the specialist who has attended him and had arranged to send him away from his wife to an asylum, at Clarissa Dalloway's party in his white tie and tails.

Then there is another strand: Clarissa's daughter, Elizabeth, who is challenging and questioning her mother's values, accepting for the moment those of her ugly, unattractive history teacher, Miss Kilman. One is confident that Elizabeth will find something very much better before long, but even Miss Kilman is better than unquestioning acceptance. Elizabeth is just at the age when a young girl often resents the fact that she is bound to grow into a woman:

> And already, even as she stood there, in her very well-cut clothes, it was beginning. . . . People were beginning to compare her to poplar trees, early dawn, hyacinths, fawns, running water, and garden lilies; and it made her life a burden to her, for she so much preferred being left alone to do what she liked in the country, but they would compare her to lilies, and she had to go to parties, and London was so dreary compared to being alone in the country with her father and the dogs.

Finally there is the party—the party that brings all the strands together and that symbolises all that Clarissa Dalloway values. Sally Seton whom we have only known from memories in the minds of Clarissa Dalloway and Peter Walsh, and who broke away from her family and said outrageous things that shocked the conventions of her youth, sweeps in uninvited. She has scarcely had time to embrace her hostess when the Prime Minister is announced and Clarissa has to leave her old friend, and Sally finds Peter Walsh. They talk about their hostess as Clarissa takes the Prime Minister around. Sally condemns her utterly:

What Sally felt was simply this. She had owed Clarissa an enormous amount. They had been friends, not acquaintances, friends, and she still saw Clarissa all in white going about the house with her hands full of flowers—to this day tobacco made her think of Bourton. But—did Peter understand?—she lacked something. Lacked what was it? She had charm; she had extraordinary charm. But . . . married Richard Dalloway? a sportsman, a man who cared only for dogs. Literally, when he came into the room he smelt of the stables. And then all this? She waved her hand.

. . . Clarissa was at heart a snob—one had to admit it, a snob. And it was that that was between them, she was convinced. Clarissa thought she had married beneath her, her husband being—she was proud of it—a miner's son. Every penny they had he had earned.

But Peter is bored by this and is seduced by the charm of Clarissa's personality into accepting her as she is.

That is my reading of this wonderful book which seems to me to be one of the great novels in the English language. The subject of it, I believe, had been suggested by what happened to a close friend of her girlhood who as they say had made 'a very suitable marriage' such as George Duckworth wanted for his sisters. But thanks largely to Vanessa and to Thoby, she had escaped to freedom and a very different marriage.

Many critics rank *To the Lighthouse* above *Mrs Dalloway* as the greatest of Virginia's novels. I do not, for the theme of her own parents and childhood seems to me less important. The characterisation may go deeper, but *Mrs Dalloway* is not only a social indictment it is an interweaving in presentation which as far as I know, is unique in literature. With these two masterpieces, the critics respectfully place *The Waves* and *The Years*. But again I differ. I turn back on the judgement of the thoughtful reasonable man who asks that the novel should comment with a certain realism upon life as we live it.

There is more to great writing—great prose writing, great story-telling, than that. There are fantasy and inspiration which rank with great poetry. Many writers have had glimpses of this (myself included) standing like urchins peeping through into the Great Top of the circus, into fairyland. Virginia is the greatest of the fantasists of our time. I am carried away by *Orlando*. It is, I think, the essence of Virginia herself. She started it as a joke, and this gave her a freedom that enraptures me. *Orlando* is also a love-letter. It has a gay teasing intimacy which puts it above that other work of fantasy, *Flush*. I love *Flush* and was lucky enough to be able to write a review of it which drew the following letter from Virginia:

> 52 Tavistock Sq
> Sunday
> Private

My dear Bunny,

You were more than generous and wholly delightful about *Flush* and Virginia last week; and I had meant to write and thank you before, but not being altogether a dog, as you justly observe, had no time to go to The London Library and prove that I'm not so inaccurate as you think. No. I'm rather proud of my facts. About license, for instance; surely I made it plain that I was referring to nature, not the Post Office? License natural to age. Well, I ask you what has that to do with the Encyclopaedia? or the Post Office, or six and eightpence? Nature's license sometimes called lust. About the working man's cottage; I agree it looks like a farm in the picture; but Mr Orion Horne calls it a working man's cottage; and he saw it; and was not a picturesque artist. Painters at that date always enlarge houses out of consideration for their owners. Such is my view as a biographer (and Oh Lord how does any one pretend to be a biographer?—) As for asphalt I admit I have my doubts; but I suspect that the Prince regent liked asphalt—asphalt seems to be implied in the Pavilion. But how could you let slip that horrid anachronism which stares at you bright red on page I don't know what? There were no pillar boxes in the year 1846. They were invented by Anthony Trollope about 1852. Don't expose me. If you do, my sales will prick like a bubble. Old gentlemen will die in fury. I could go on, but will stop having I hope partly vindicated my claim to truth speaking. Yes; the last paragraph as originally written was simply Queen Victoria dying all over again.—Flush remembered his entire past in Lytton's best manner; but I cut it out, when he was not there to see the joke. But what a good critic you are—lots of the things you said I think of in the watches of the night; they stick like burs, whereas the others, save Desmond, run off my coat like water.

Your affectionate old English springer spaniel

> Virginia

There was another side to Viginia as a writer. She was a literary critic of the front rank. In her two volumes, *The Common Reader* and the posthumous volume *Granite*, she shows that she was not the daughter of Leslie Stephen for nothing. Indeed she was sensitive to worlds of which he was ignorant. The wish of her godfather James Russell Lowell that her heredity might blossom and bear fruit was abundantly fulfilled. She was a scholar whose critical works reveal the balanced orderly powers of a first-rate intelligence. At any moment she could write a biographical sketch, or an article in *The Times Literary Supplement* marshalling her facts and delivering her judgement with ease and wit. In her novels and stories the originality of her approach, the beauty of her language and the associations which echo poetry like the murmur of the waves, evoked for us by a shell clasped to the ear, make Virginia one of the half-dozen great women writers, and perhaps the least like a man of all.

John Maynard Keynes
and Lydia Lopokova

John Maynard Keynes and Lydia Lopokova

He stood in the doorway, looking at me out of beautiful dark blue eyes, without surprise, quiet, friendly, undemonstrative, and apparently knowing who I was before I spoke.

'Geoffrey was sent off to France last night. Come in and have some tea.'

The news was a blow. I had hoped to go out with him as a bacteriologist, or dispenser, or even as his batman, and it had not occurred to me, or I think to Maynard's brother, Geoffrey Keynes, that my idea of joining an R.A.M.C. field hospital at the last moment, without training, was fantastic. It was a few days after the fourth of August 1914, and we were at war with Germany.

I followed Maynard into the beautiful room on the north side of Brunswick Square, with its mural of a street scene, a cabhorse fallen between the shafts of a hansom cab and a group of cockneys looking on. I knew the room well. It was Adrian Stephen's house, and I used to go there on Thursdays to play poker.

Maynard told me that he had succeeded in raising enough money to enable the Hungarian poet, Ferenc Békássy, to leave England the night before. The banks were all shut owing to a moratorium, and Békássy was anxious to return to Hungary to fight against Russia. Like Rupert Brooke and others, he was in love with Noel Olivier, and it was through her that I had got to know him. War had not been declared between Britain and the Austro-Hungarian Empire until that morning.

I said that I thought Maynard should have refused to find the money on the grounds that he was sending a friend to his death and strengthening the enemy forces.

Maynard lay back in his armchair sipping a cup of tea, absolutely relaxed, and listened to me. He disagreed. He said he had used every

JOHN MAYNARD KEYNES

argument to persuade Békássy not to go—but having failed to persuade him, it was not the part of a friend to impose his views by force, by refusing help. He respected Békássy's freedom to choose, though he regretted his choice. My second reason was ridiculous: what was one man in many millions?

I agreed with Maynard that friendship was more important than patriotism, but asked him if he would lend the money to a friend, who contemplated suicide, to buy poison. Maynard replied that in certain circumstances he would lend the money—if it were a free choice, made by a sane man after due reflection, for compelling reasons. Békássy was killed not long afterwards in the Carpathians. Maynard had his name included among those members of King's College, Cambridge, killed in the war, which is carved in King's College Chapel. But it stands alone, on the other face of the pillar from the long list of British losses.

From this discussion of ethics, Maynard went on to talk about the war. Much to my surprise I discovered that he was optimistic. He told me that he was quite certain that the war could not last much more than a year, and that the belligerent countries could not be ruined by it. The world, he explained, was enormously rich, but its wealth was, fortunately, of a kind that could not be realised for war purposes, since it was in the form of capital equipment for making things which were useless for waging war. When all the available wealth had been used up, which he thought would take about a year, the Powers would have to make peace. We could not use Lancashire cotton factories to blockade Germany, Germany could not use toymakers' factories to equip her armies. These views were stated with extraordinary clarity and absolute conviction, and I unhesitatingly believed them. What is more, I went on believing them, in spite of all the evidence to the contrary, until the spring of 1915.

I had had thoughts of enlisting—not from patriotic motives, but because I felt that the war was a great human experience which I ought not to miss. But since it would be such a short war it would be silly to spend it being drilled on a barrack square. And I had just won a scholarship to continue my research.

I did not see Maynard again for five months, when he invited me to dinner at the Café Royal before Mrs Bell's party at 46 Gordon Square. It was my real introduction to 'Bloomsbury'. That stratum of London society was not a homogeneous whole. It was split—much as the Highlands of Scotland are split by Loch Linnhe, Loch Lochy and Loch Ness—into more remote and more accessible portions. Duncan Grant,

JOHN MAYNARD KEYNES

Maynard Keynes, Harry Norton, Roger Fry and I owed allegiance to Vanessa. Leonard, Lytton, Desmond MacCarthy and Morgan Forster to Virginia. Duncan and Leonard would not have met so frequently, nor would Lytton and 'Pozzo'—to give Maynard his Strachey nickname—if it had not been for the meetings between Vanessa and Virginia. Clive Bell belonged to both camps. Carrington and I can be described as appendages. I was intimate with her and Lytton, but not with Virginia and Leonard. They were all old friends, but it was the love of the two sisters for each other which kept all of them together.

I cannot speak of Maynard as a political economist, or as a mathematician. I can only describe him as a most generous friend and as an author whose writing is neglected because of his other outstanding talents. I can only catalogue his acts of kindness and hope the reader will judge his character from them.

I am not sure when Maynard went to the Treasury, but on hearing of it, I wrote him a letter, the gist of which was that when the professional politicians had got themselves and the country into a sufficiently bad mess, they called in men with first-class brains to get them out of it. But when these intellectuals had succeeded, their reward would be to be sent back to their university cloisters, and never allowed to rearrange the world so that the mess did not recur.

Though my words were crude and prejudiced they were not what most young men of my age would have written, and Maynard was pleased with the letter and I think agreed with it, but the task now was to get out of the mess. It was to be a longer job than he had thought, and the aftermath was to be the Peace to End Peace, in trying to prevent which Maynard played the noblest part.

Maynard was never a revolutionary, because he knew how precarious is our civilisation, and that it is maintained by an intellectual élite that must constantly recruit itself from the people, and must be ready to modify its actions with every generation, if humane standards are not to be overwhelmed by the violence of the mob.

By the end of 1915 I had become a pacifist; the work I was doing in France had come to an end, there was talk of conscription in England, and I was undecided whether to return to England or to join the Friends Italian Ambulance Unit in which my father was working as a hospital orderly.

Maynard, who was in a position to know the Government's intentions, wrote and told me that conscription was very unlikely and that I should return. I might get a job translating Russian. I came back, conscription was introduced, and Maynard came to the Military Service Appeal Tribunal to support my claim to exemption on conscientious grounds, which was refused. Afterwards it was granted by the Central Tribunal on condition that I did work on a farm.

Duncan Grant and I then became agricultural labourers living in an old farmhouse in Sussex rented by Vanessa Bell. Maynard was a constant visitor, and in the three years which followed I got to know him well. He would arrive in the evening for the weekend, driven in a hired car from Lewes, tired out, but with a bulging Treasury bag, and stay in bed till lunchtime next morning, by which time the waste-paper basket would be full of the papers he had dealt with.

When he came down he was a free man. One of his favourite occupations at Charleston was weeding the paths. It was not the ordinary beheading the weeds with a hoe and leaving the roots. Maynard would kneel on a small mat, and with his pocket knife extirpate every trace of grass, plantain, dandelion, or whatever formed the green carpet over the path. Naturally progress was slow, but the task was resumed on every visit, and a belt of clean gravel a yard or two long, terminating in a stretch of lush vegetation, marked the extent of Maynard's labours. This weeding was a therapeutic exercise, which gave him a spiritual renewal from the frustrations of work at the Treasury.

On Sunday morning I would sometimes go and squat beside him and gossip. If Clive or another visitor were there we would often go for a walk on the Downs. Once, on Firle Beacon, a strong south-east wind was blowing, and the rumble of the guns across the Channel was loud. Someone remarked on it, and I said that it was because of the wind. Maynard took me up, and declared that as sound travelled through the ether, the wind could make no difference.

I should have replied: 'I can't hear you Maynard. The wind is blowing the words out of your mouth.' But I only contradicted Maynard and said that he was wrong—sound waves travelled through matter.

'Bunny doesn't agree with Cambridge scientists about the diffusion of sound,' remarked Maynard, and the party hurried on, leaving me suffocating with rage.

I know that this anecdote is hardly to be credited, but it is a most vivid memory.

In the spring of 1918 Duncan learned that the pictures in Degas' collection were going to be auctioned in Paris. There were Cézannes, Manets, Delacroixs, and so on. He thought that some should be bought for the National Gallery and told Maynard to pull the necessary strings. Maynard threw himself into the plan, and after consulting Holmes, the director of the Gallery, astonished Bonar Law, the Chancellor of the Exchequer, by recommending a purchase.

It was, he said, the first time that Maynard had recommended spending money. The sale coincided with a financial congress and with the German breakthrough and rout of General Gough's Fifth Army. As a result the prices were low. Holmes wore a false beard so as not to be recognised by the Paris dealers. Unfortunately for the National Gallery, Lord Curzon, one of the Trustees, forbade the purchase of a Cézanne, and not all the money allocated by the Treasury was spent.

However the Renoir of the Umbrellas and the large Manet of the execution of the Emperor Maximilian in Mexico were secured.

Duncan, Vanessa and I had just finished dinner at Charleston when the front door was pushed open and Maynard appeared out of the darkness. He had crossed the Channel in a destroyer, and Austen Chamberlain, who had a house in Sussex, had dropped him at Swingate, where the private road to Charleston meets the Lewes–Eastbourne road. He had left his suitcase in the ditch, and it contained a small Cézanne which he had bought for himself.

Duncan and I ran down and lugged it back. The excitement was intense as the little panel—a still life of apples—was produced and Maynard told us the story of his adventures, in which the picture sale played a greater part than the financial congress, or the halt of the exhausted Germans after their breakthrough.

Maynard's preoccupation was to persuade the American Treasury to make loans direct to the French. Early in the war, they gave loans to England, part of which we passed on to France. Maynard succeeded in getting loans made to France without any English responsibility.

One day at lunch Vanessa announced that she had engaged an old man at Firle to work in the garden at Charleston. Until then I had assumed responsibility for it. It was the only way in which I could repay Vanessa for giving me free board and lodging. On hearing that she had engaged a gardener, I rushed from the table and burst into tears in the garden. Maynard followed me, and I explained to him that I was being made into a complete parasite. The last shreds of my self-respect were being taken from me. Maynard walked up and down with me, explaining that it was impossible for me to do a week's hard work as a farm labourer—with overtime in the summer—and also to cultivate the Charleston garden. It was enough that I kept many hives of bees and provided the household with almost unlimited honey. I had made a success of them and had repaid him for the loan to buy more hives.

For a good half-hour Maynard reasoned with me and consoled me, leaving his lunch to get cold. Such kindness and sympathy were characteristic of him. When Mark Gertler waylaid and assaulted Lytton Strachey after a party at the Hutchinsons', it was Maynard who took him by the arm and led him away, reasoning with him and consoling him for his frantic jealousy.

One day at Charleston, Maynard burst out with a piece of news. We had decided to overturn the Bolshevik Revolution. The Communists under Lenin and Trotsky were threatened by Admiral Kolchak advancing through Siberia. And now we had landed an army at Murmansk, had set up a Government of Russian liberals at Archangel and would soon crush the Bolsheviks. Maynard was cock-a-hoop.

I knew what Constance would think of such an adventure, and I told him that if anything was needed to settle Lenin in power, it was foreign intervention. The plan which he greeted with such excitement and delight was doomed to failure. Every step that our soldiers took towards Moscow would be hampered by the opposition of the Russian peasants. We could no more overturn the Revolution than Napoleon could conquer Russia. Every Russian liberal who supported us would be regarded as a traitor who had sold himself to the foreigner.

Events were to prove that Constance's assessment of the situation— for it was hers not mine—was right. Some months later, Maynard admitted that he had been mistaken.

He depended very much on the good opinion of his friends, particularly on that of Duncan and Vanessa. Once he had taken anyone to his heart, he was a friend for life, however much their paths might diverge. But as the war went on, his friends became more and more critical, and there was a painful scene when they attacked him for the part he was playing. They were pacifists whose opinions were often right in the main, but they were ignorant of the political undercurrents and the intentions of the Government. Maynard knew all the secrets and was unable to use his knowledge in argument to refute ignorant attacks. He could never say: 'That just isn't so. The facts are . . .' For the facts during a war are kept secret. I think that Duncan was the only one of his intimate friends and critics who realised this.

Everything was transformed by his resignation during the Peace Conference. He had realised in time what was being done in the Peace Treaty. It outraged his sense of honour, his sense of humanity, his knowledge of what was possible. He resigned and wrote *The Economic Consequences of the Peace*. In doing so he became a moral force.

His resignation was due not only to his intelligence and his clear-sightedness, but also to the ethos of the Cambridge in which he grew up, and to the influence of the friends whom he loved, whose judgements he respected and whose basic unworldliness he shared. It is because he did not betray his own and their values that he was able to go on and have a continually increasing influence.

I have been told that Lytton Strachey persuaded Maynard to keep the sentence in which he wrote that President Wilson's hands were lacking in sensitiveness and finesse, which he had intended to omit. Incidentally that sentence tells us at least as much about Maynard as it does about the President. It reinforces what I shall say later. I think a comparison between Lytton's description of Gladstone and Maynard's of Lloyd George, written two or three years later, shows Lytton's influence. Each of them was writing about the complex character of a Prime Minister, but Maynard was drawing from life. Lytton wrote:

In the physical world there are no chimeras. But man is more various than nature; was Mr Gladstone, perhaps, a chimera of the spirit? Did his very essence lie in the confusion of incompatibles? His very essence? It eludes the hand that seems to grasp it. One is baffled as his political opponents were baffled fifty years ago. The soft serpent coils harden into quick strength that has vanished leaving only emptiness and perplexity behind. Speech was the fibre of his being and when he spoke the ambiguity of ambiguity was revealed. . . . But here also was a contradiction. In spite of the involutions of his intellect and the contortions of his spirit it is impossible not to perceive a strain of *naïveté* in Mr Gladstone. . . . His very egoism was simple-minded: through all the labyrinth? Ah, the thread might lead there through those wandering mazes at last. Only with the last corner turned, the last step taken, the explorer might find that he was looking down into the gulf of a crater. The flame shot out on every side scorching and brilliant, but in the midst there was a darkness.

And here is Maynard on Lloyd George:

How can I convey to the reader who does not know him any just impression of this extraordinary figure of our time? This syren, this goat-footed bard, half-human visitor to our age from the hag-ridden magic and enchanted woods of Celtic antiquity? One catches in his company that flavour of final purposelessness, inner irresponsibility, existence outside and away from our Saxon good and evil, mixed with cunning, remorselessness, love of power, that lend fascination, enthralment and terror to the fair-seeming magicians of North

European folklore. . . . Lloyd George is rooted in nothing, he is void and without content; he lives and feeds on his immediate surroundings; he is an instrument and a player at the same time which plays on the company and is played on by them too; he is a prism, as I have heard him described, which collects light and distorts it and is most brilliant if the light comes from many quarters at once; a vampire and a medium in one.

Maynard would not have written that passage *in quite that way* if he had not read *Eminent Victorians*. But how much better it is! How much better written, for one thing. There is no hand seeming to grasp an elusive essence—a messy image. And it does convey something genuine and felt whereas all Lytton tells us is that Gladstone was contradictory and incomprehensible. Nevertheless I believe that Lytton's influence on Maynard was a wholly good one. It tempted him to be more indiscreet than he was by nature: to have the courage to print what he would have said in conversation. In Maynard's best writing there is an element inevitably absent from Lytton at his best: a *visual* quality. Maynard had the enormous advantage of writing of what he had seen with his own eyes, and those beautiful deep blue eyes noticed every detail. All through the *Essays in Biography* there are passages in which his eyes have been caught by what is significant and which tell everything in a dozen words. 'Charlie Chaplin with the forehead of Shakespeare' is the best description of Einstein.

Again the portrait of Clemenceau in 'The Council of Four' could only have been drawn by someone who had studied him from life and had eyes for every significant detail. It is not only that Maynard had the enormous advantage of having met and talked with most of the men he was writing about, but that he had a much more acute visual sense. He cared more for pictures than Lytton and learned more from Duncan Grant and Vanessa Bell than Lytton ever learned from Carrington. Maynard's Clemenceau has the solidity of a portrait by Ingres. There he sits on his brocaded chair, his hands gloved, in his thick black square-tailed coat of good broadcloth, tired and patient, listening to the Anglo-Saxon humbug, and Maynard has eyes that see that: 'His boots were of thick black leather, very good, but of a country style, and sometimes fastened in front, curiously by a buckle instead of laces.' And as another example of his keeping down to earth, how significant is this sentence in his delightful and loving account of Mary Paley Marshall:

Every morning till close on her ninetieth year, when, to her extreme dissatisfaction, her doctor prohibited her (partly at her friends' instigation, but more on account of the dangers of the Cambridge traffic even to the most able-bodied than to any failure of her physical powers), she bicycled the considerable distance from Madingley Road to the Library . . . wearing, as she always did, the sandals which were a legacy of her pre-Raphaelite period sixty years before.

And of Ysidro Edgeworth he wrote: 'Quotations from the Greek tread on the heels of the differential calculus and the philistine reader can scarcely tell whether it is a line of Homer or a mathematical abstraction which is in the course of integration.'

Like Lytton, Maynard was often most profound when he was wittiest. For example, he visited General Haking of the Armistice Commission, who had installed himself, his wife and two marriageable daughters in what had been Ludendorff's villa, until the collapse of Germany, amid a semicircle of pine trees. In this Wagnerian setting General Haking's A.D.C. and his fellow-subalterns had imported a pack of hounds. *The Times* arrived regularly on the breakfast table. But for Maynard the ghost of Ludendorff haunted the spot: he imagined him unbuckling his bright breast-plate—a figure in opera—and calling to the soughing pines. And he adds: 'Miss Bates had vanquished Brünnhilde and Mr Weston's foot was firmly planted on the neck of Wotan.'

That joke is sheer genius. It symbolises and sums up the unbridgeable gulf between England and Germany which makes it next to impossible for the countries to understand each other. On the basis of that joke a composer and librettist might compose a very amusing light opera.

Later on in 'Dr Melchior' Maynard returns to the same theme when he describes a Conference presided over by Admiral Sir Rosslyn Wemyss who, goggling at Maynard with the look of a sea-sick porpoise, astonished the Germans by 'total abandonment of the faintest attempt to keep up appearances of knowing what this Conference was about, coupled with his supreme self-possession and unassailable, as it were, social superiority, like a humorous and good-natured duchess presiding over the financial business of a local charity—which somehow made *them*, so serious and pompous, seem to be a little absurd.'

'Dr Melchior: A Defeated Enemy' is the finest of Maynard's writings. It combines deep personal feeling, a passion for humanity and justice, the unravelling of all the tangled threads in the negotiations, with and an almost uncanny observation of tiny but very significant detail. It is so real and so profoundly moving that I would compare it not to any other piece of historical writing that I know, but to a chapter from some great work of the imagination—by Tolstoy perhaps. It is a work of art. Perhaps it is the best of Maynard's writings because it was composed to be read to the small group of old friends to whom he could reveal everything in his nature.

Maynard himself would not have been happy if I did not mention his mastery of historical detail and the carefulness of his research in such matters as the explanation of character by the influence of heredity and environment which he employed to put each of his subjects into his social and intellectual frame. In such work he was meticulous. His greatness as a writer is not only because of his intellectual eminence and versatility; it is also moral.

Vanessa depended upon him and constantly sought his advice. Once I wanted to ask Maynard a question and went up to his bedroom in Gordon Square, as he usually did not appear till mid-day. The bed was empty but the door of the bathroom was ajar.

'Is that you Bunny? Come in.'

Maynard was lying soaking in a hot bath and Vanessa was sitting on a chair asking him advice about some practical problem. This did not strike me as unusual at the time.

Such casual indifference to the conventions did not survive Maynard's marriage to Lydia Lopokova. At the first sight of Lydia, I fell in love—the love of the moth for the star. She was dancing in *The Good-Humoured Ladies* with Massine. It was a love full of respect and of tenderness. For though her body was obviously as strong and as elastic as whalebone, she was, I knew, vulnerable: her spirit sensitive and responsive.

That I should ever meet her, speak to her, or even gaze in adoration, except from the gallery, seemed impossible. But actually the miracle came about at once, when Lady Ottoline Morrell pushed ahead of me, and I followed, to Massine's dressing-room, and then Lydia appeared, vigorous, laughing, talking and wiping greasepaint off her forehead.

I saw her again at parties given by Clive and Vanessa. Duncan Grant and she appreciated each other from the first.

I only got to know her after she had married Maynard—it seemed to me that they were ideally suited. He amused and protective, Lydia turning constantly to him for the sympathy and approbation which were always forthcoming.

One day Maynard asked me if I would collaborate in—or ghost—an article which Lydia was to write for the *Evening News*. It was delightful.

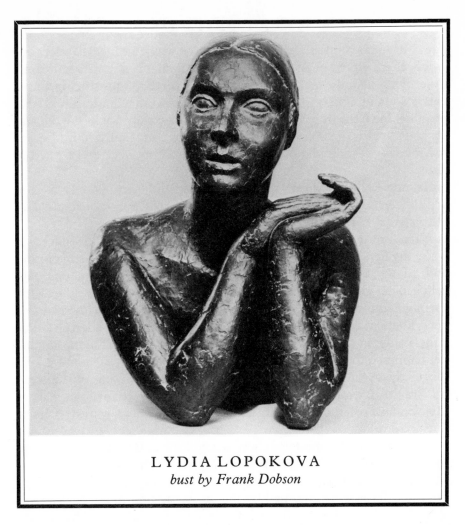

LYDIA LOPOKOVA
bust by Frank Dobson

We talked it over. I think I gave Lydia confidence—but I hardly wrote anything myself—the whole point seemed to me not Lydia's ideas about cookery but her enchanting use of the English language. I haven't seen the article for forty years or so, but I remember that she began her recipe for sorrel soup with the words: 'You can find a bland grass growing in the fields. . .' 'Bland' is the last adjective I should use to describe the sharp acidity of sorrel, but I left the readers of the *Evening News* to search for this grass before they could melt it in butter thickened with flour, and then stir in milk and cream with an egg yolk liaison at the last minute.

When I owned an aeroplane with Jamie Hamilton (we flew it on alternate weekends) Maynard invited me to Tilton and I flew down. I

143

knew the fields round Charleston and Tilton well, but I had to select one where there were not any cattle and not too many trees. I spent some time flying round, incidentally scaring Roger Fry into driving into a gatepost, and finally landed in the field behind Charleston. I was pegging down the little Klemm, when a car drove up. Lydia got out and rushed towards me followed by Maynard and Sam Courtauld, who was my fellow-guest. Lydia flung her arms round my neck and turned to Sam.

'Is not Boony a hero?' she exclaimed, and getting only a faint acquiescence, repeated, 'Boony, you are my hero.' Sam Courtauld gave me a sympathetic smile.

What can I say about that weekend? We three men rejoiced in watching her, hearing her eager voice. And then, just as the sun recedes and all the colour changes—like that—a look of sadness, of doubt eclipsed her gay vitality. What was she thinking? Was she feeling lost in a strange country? She turned to Maynard, and a look from him restored her. There was the tough side, too. She kept that wonderful elastic body fit doing high kicks over the bar in her room at Tilton, holding her slippered toe and turning in a slow pirouette upon the point. . . No longer the great ballerina, she delighted us by her acting. But instead of 'Bravo!' I would have liked to call: 'Loppy—we love you.' After the applause of thousands in all the capitals, there were the lucky few.

I have been asked about 'her non-acceptance by Bloomsbury'. Unless that is a polite euphemism for Vanessa's violent opposition to Maynard's marriage, I do not know what is meant. Clive Bell and Duncan Grant were charmed by her from the first moment. Vanessa always opposed the marriages of her friends, although she herself accepted the social convenience of being a married woman. But her opposition to Maynard's marriage was more violent and embittered than usual, because she had come to feel over the years that he was part of her household. Duncan was acutely distressed by Vanessa's hostility to the marriage, and when I once referred to it, wept and could not reply.

Thanks to Maynard's understanding and affection, he did not show resentment, and time as always, healed the wound. The fact of Lydia's becoming a member of the Memoir Club helped. It also very soon became obvious that Lydia and Maynard were complementary. It was due to Duncan Grant that Maynard started his collection of pictures, but it was due to Lydia that he made ballet and opera a national concern, and that he got the Arts Theatre built in Cambridge. The Arts Council is his posthumous memorial.

One of my memories of Lydia is at parties in 46 Gordon Square, singing Victorian drawing-room ballads—set to music by Major Bartle Grant, Duncan's father. With what a pleading voice and pathetic expression did she utter the absurd lines:

'Oh, my earrings, my earrings:
They have fallen down the well
And how to tell my Mirza
I cannot, cannot tell.

When Francis Birrell and I were planning to start a bookshop, Augustine Birrell consulted Maynard. His advice proved embarrassing. C. K. Ogden had made a great success of the *Cambridge Magazine* during the last years of the war, by publishing extracts from the press of neutral countries not otherwise available. Maynard suggested that Ogden should enter into partnership with us—he would provide the business acumen in which Francis and I were noticeably lacking. Ogden was willing, but the terms of partnership had to be agreed.

Francis disliked Ogden so much that he said he would abandon the enterprise rather than become Ogden's partner. It was a situation which required diplomatic skill. I met Ogden to discuss the terms of partnership.

Ogden had acquired the stock of a bankrupt bookseller in Cambridge. He proposed that the new firm should take this over as part of his investment. I professed delighted agreement. It was a good beginning, and encouraged by my imbecility Ogden opened his mouth wider. He proposed that the remainder of his shares were to be paid for by full-page advertisements in the *Cambridge Magazine*. Frankie and I were to pay for our shares in cash. I got Ogden to put his proposals on paper, and we parted highly delighted with each other. It often pays to be thought half-witted. I knew that it was useless for me to oppose Maynard's proposal that we should take Ogden into partnership. He who had put forward the plan must tell old Mr Birrell that it would not do. I therefore wrote to Maynard, enclosing Ogden's grotesque proposals and asking him whether these were terms of partnership which he approved.

Naturally they were not, and Frankie and I were free to pursue our own plans.

A conference of bankers was taking place in Italy, and Maynard, who was on holiday with Duncan, took him to the house of the very cultivated Director of the Bank of Italy. Maynard was surprised to find himself led off by the Director's wife and shown the pictures on the walls. On coming back to the main reception room, he found Duncan holding forth about the financial situation to a group of bankers roaring with laughter at what they thought were Signor Keynes's brilliant paradoxes.

Maynard's resignation because of the unrealistic and unjust demands for reparations in the Peace Treaty and his publication of the *Economic Consequences of the Peace* put him in a unique position among world economists. He became a leading figure in the Liberal party. When the Liberal *Nation* and the Socialist *New Statesman* were amalgamated, a new Literary Editor was required, and after Leonard Woolf had refused the job, it was offered to me. I enjoyed the work, but got on badly both with Kingsley Martin, the Editor, and with Roberts, the Manager. When I took a month's holiday to write *Beany-Eye*, Kingsley appointed Raymond Mortimer Literary Editor in my place without informing me. I appealed to Maynard. As a result I was paid £500 compensation for wrongful dismissal and given the job of writing the column *Books in General* at the salary I had drawn as Literary Editor. This arrangement worked perfectly until the Second World War began in September 1939.

Gibbon's library had been discovered in Switzerland and was to be auctioned at Sotheby's. Maynard produced the catalogue when Aldous Huxley and I had had dinner with him and Lydia, and we went through it saying which of Gibbon's books we should most like to possess. I chose Hooker's *Ecclesiastical Polity*. Neither Aldous nor Maynard knew anything about Hooker, and they were interested when I claimed that he was one of the finest prose writers and that the Church of England had been built upon Hooker's ideas. I liked to think of Gibbon reading Hooker before writing his magnificent attack upon Christianity.

A few days later I received an enormous parcel, Hooker's *Ecclesiastical Polity* in elephant folio with Gibbon's bookplate and a pencilled inscription from Maynard.

This was by no means the last of his generous gifts to me. I had been elected to the Memoir Club, and one evening before the reading began Duncan and I began talking about our relative poverty. I said that I had not the money to educate my two sons, Duncan said that he had to support his mother.

JOHN MAYNARD KEYNES

This conversation was overheard by Maynard, and soon afterwards I got a letter from him saying that he wanted to help Duncan financially, but that Duncan would only accept the money if Maynard were to help me. To Duncan Maynard said that I would only accept if Duncan did.

The result was that Maynard made two convenants: one to pay my sons' school fees and the other to help support Duncan's mother. It was typical of Maynard's kindness and generosity as well as of the subtlety with which he linked his two benefactions together.

He was one of the most brilliant talkers I have known. He would pounce on any remark which interested him, extend it, develop it. At the Treasury his room was opposite that of Lord Catto. This led to his being given the name of Doggo. And in his unswerving fidelity to his old friends and his affection for them there was something canine. And so was his gift for pouncing and seizing the essential and the gundog's nose which led him to recognise it instantly.

In this portrait sketch I have dwelt on his mistakes which were obvious, whereas his great achievements demand expert appreciation.

But they have led to his brilliance as a biographer being overlooked. He had the advantage over Lytton Strachey of having known the men he was writing about personally. He wrote of all with affection but with a delightful wit, and could sum up a man in a sentence. If I were to sum up Maynard it would be 'Affection, understanding, flashing intelligence.'

Lytton Strachey and Carrington

Lytton Strachey and Carrington

We walked along the edge of a cornfield on a footpath from Wissett Lodge towards Halesworth in Suffolk. It was the early summer of 1916. Lytton began talking, and, as we were in single file, it was difficult to hear him. I stopped and, though it meant breaking down some of the stalks of unripe corn, walked beside him. He was telling me that he had been invited by Barbara Hiles to go to her parents' holiday cottage in Wales to chaperon her and Lieutenant Nicholas Bagenal of the Irish Guards, who was on leave and in love with her. Lytton's presence would soothe her mother's feelings of propriety. Carrington, a fellow-student of Barbara's at the Slade, would be the fourth member of the party. Lytton then said that he thought he was in love with Carrington. This was told me in a hesitating mixture of eagerness and deprecation. He had burst out because he needed to make a confidence. And then came the fear that he had been indiscreet. I was asked to swear not to repeat what he had told me to either Duncan or Vanessa. Duncan would tell Vanessa, and she would relate it in a letter to Virginia, and the fat would be in the fire. Ottoline would hear of it, which would be fatal. I did not breathe a word of Lytton's secret. He spent a fortnight in Wales, and when Nicholas Bagenal's leave was up, he and Carrington went on a tour of the West Country together.

Henry Lamb's famous portrait of Lytton in the Tate Gallery reminds one of an etiolated plant soon to die for lack of fresh air, light and the watering-can. There were moments when Lytton was exhausted, and the strain of sitting for hours to Henry may explain his languor. But Lytton was often active, going for long walks on the Downs or in his own words bounding along and whisking from Square to Circus.

He was very gay, enjoyed what he saw, and was a delightful companion, eager to explore. He particularly enjoyed jaunts to cities with eighteenth-century or Regency architecture: Wells, Bath, Winchester, Salisbury, Southampton, with a companion who shared his

LYTTON STRACHEY
bust by Stephen Tomlin

taste for those periods and could contribute ideas of his own in conversation.

For much of his life he was ill—there were times when he was muffled in shawls and drank his Horlick's malted milk at stated intervals. Then he would suddenly revive, go to parties, seek adventures and climb hills. To be with him then was a delight and an education. I was once his companion in a jaunt which took in Salisbury, Stonehenge and Southampton. He seized at once on essentials. The human sacrifices at Stonehenge, for example.

Just as the picture of Lytton as an exhausted lily left over from the nineties is false, so is the view of Carrington as a country hoyden occupied in setting ducks' eggs under broody hens. She was a reader with a taste of her own before she ever met Lytton. It was she who introduced him to the books of W. H. Hudson and Norman Douglas. After the stay in the Welsh cottage, Lytton wrote to me:

I enjoyed the Welsh fortnight very much indeed. Barbara managed the cottage and the cooking and the whole menage with the greatest skill. I had gone expecting to find bleakness and some absence of comfort, but everything was perfectly civilised, parquet floors, spring beds, air cushions, delicious meals, and an old hag to wash up . . . I don't think there was a single day without rain. But there were warm intervals during which we sprang up into the mountain fastnesses with great agility. . . Nick was really charming—his gaiety of spirits never ceased. It will be horrible if he is forced back into that murderous cesspool. As for Carrington—we seemed to see a great deal of each other. But this let me remark at once—my attitude throughout in relation to all has been one of immaculate chastity, whatever the conduct of others may have been.

In the same letter he wrote:

I was in Bath for a day or two with Carrington. Do you know it? Really it's a most charming town. How one bounds along those elegant streets and whisks from Square to Circus and Circus to Crescent! One almost begins to feel that one's on high heels, and embroidery sprouts on one's waistcoat. And then, the infectious enthusiasm of my youthful companion . . . you smile but you are mistaken.

That infectious enthusiasm became a more and more delightful background to Lytton's life, while he maintained the façade of being entirely homosexual.

He was alarmed lest his liaison with an apparently unsophisticated young woman should excite the malicious hilarity of Lady Ottoline

LYTTON STRACHEY EXPLAINING GIBBON
TO CARRINGTON
photograph by Barbara Bagenal

Morrell—a hilarity spiced perhaps with jealousy? He had to keep up his reputation of being indifferent to, and rather horrified by, attractive young women. There were solid reasons also. Carrington's parents had to be kept in ignorance, and Gertler's jealousy not excited . . . It was also convenient for Lytton to know that he was always a welcome guest at Lady Ottoline's country house. He could put up with only being given one egg for breakfast . . . it would be impossible to stay at Garsington if he were to be constantly teased about having fallen a victim to the charms of a countrified girl.

However, the attachment grew and could not be concealed. Although Carrington agreed to have sexual relations with Gertler the result was unfortunate. When I was walking up Haverstock Hill with Lytton—though I cannot remember where we were going—he told me that Gertler's insensitive violence and clumsiness had made all physical love hateful to Carrington, and he doubted if she would get over the repulsion that it gave her.

In contrast to Gertler's violence and demands, Lytton showed the sympathy and understanding which were so characteristic of him, and

153

coming when she was heartbroken by the death of her younger brother, bound her to him closer than ever. I myself had twice experienced Lytton's intuitive realisation that I was in the blackest despair and his ability to restore my courage in a few words. On the first occasion I was alone in Paris, enraged because Duncan Grant had been expelled as 'an anarchist', though he had been asked to design the dresses for *Twelfth Night* by Copeau in a production sponsored by the French Government. My fury had been redoubled by the news that *The Rainbow* by D. H. Lawrence had been suppressed.

Lytton wrote to tell me that I was living in the attic of the house where Voltaire had lived as a young poet, and where he had died after conquering the rulers both of this world and the next. I was to think of that life and take courage. In the same letter he introduced me to Jane Harrison, the greatest Greek scholar of her time, who was living in the same building and studying Russian in her old age.

On the second occasion we went for a walk when I was working as a farm labourer in Sussex during the First World War. I was thinking that I was turning into a clod. I should never achieve anything myself, and in ten years' time I should be an embittered cynic who had once known a few interesting people. After we had walked for half a mile in silence, Lytton said: 'Don't despair. Remember that Sterne was an ordinary country parson until he was forty-five. Then he sat down and wrote *Tristram Shandy*.' I repeated his words often to myself. I was thirty before I was recognised as an original writer, and Lytton himself was thirty-eight before he achieved fame as an author.

In an emotional crisis I would seek advice from Maynard Keynes on practical matters. When I spoke of my feelings it was to discuss their results on my own and other peoples' lives. But with Lytton I could explain them and analyse their causes, and he would always be ready to listen without impatience, and we would end with gentle laughter at the inevitable absurdity of the human heart.

In 1918 Lytton struck a new note, reviving biography as an art, for it had sunk into an exercise in piety, laborious for the author and tedious for the reader. Lytton changed the perspective in which the Victorians were viewed. Whether Dr Arnold had short or long legs can now only be discovered by the exhumation of his skeleton, but after the publication of *Eminent Victorians* his ghost could no longer use them to bestride the educational world. The Victorians shrank in stature when Lytton wrote of them, but in becoming smaller they became alive, able to excite our sympathy and our pity. We realised that the waxworks in Madame Tussaud's had once been real and extraordinarily interesting people. Lytton's method in achieving this transformation was not simply to survey his specimens through the wrong end of his opera glasses, but to pick out salient trifles: the dirt in the ears of Italian Cardinals or Gordon's brandies and sodas early in the day—much resented when first alleged by Lytton, but since fully confirmed by the evidence of Solomon Reinach, and generally admired twenty years later in the case of Winston Churchill, though he dispensed with the soda.

Yet, partly because of his assumed detachment, partly because of his wit, the reader often feels that Lytton's judgements are 'slanted', like the B.B.C. foreign services in wartime. Too much emphasis in one place, while another aspect has been skated over or ignored, shows that Lytton was very much a propagandist. Virginia Woolf wrote in her diary: 'Then he told me how he lived for ambition; he wants influence not fame; . . . he wants to deal little words that poison vast monsters of falsehood. This I declared to be unattainable. But I believe it to be what he wishes.'

It was Voltaire's ambition also and Galileo's achievement, and it is perhaps the reason why he never carried out his original intention of writing parallel lives of those eminent Victorians whom he whole-heartedly admired. Darwin, Faraday and Lister might have been his choice. Had they been written, such lives would have been comparable to Maynard's lives of the founders of political economy at Cambridge. Lytton knew that he was not equipped to explain their contributions to knowledge.

Contrariwise Maynard should have written a life of Marx and an assessment of *Das Kapital*.

Soon Lytton's relationship with Carrington had been established. She had broken off with Gertler, and they were living together at the Mill House, Tidmarsh, the rent of which was paid by Lytton's close friends: Harry Norton, Saxon Sydney-Turner, Maynard Keynes and Lytton's brother, Oliver, who had just returned from India.

The immediate success of *Eminent Victorians* made such an arrangement appear ridiculous. But at the same time the sponsors of the Mill House, Tidmarsh were felt to have the right to stay whenever it suited them and were indeed always welcome as they were at Ham Spray to which a move was made soon after Carrington's marriage to Ralph Partridge.

Each of these houses Carrington was able to transform into an extension of her personality. Their unique quality and beauty were created round her image of Lytton.

His world of a library with shelves filled with precious books, of a sitting-room with pictures by Duncan Grant, rare china, sofas and cushions, of a dining-room with beautiful furniture—all were chosen with or by Carrington, all harmonised and combined to illustrate her taste and character, and her powers as an artist and a decorator.

But beside the rooms created for Lytton and visitors there was a string of others which were her special province. The kitchen, of course, and the still-room where she made country wines. Her cowslip wine was nectar, her sloe gin unequalled. Then the jams, bottled fruit and vegetables, chutneys, pickles, preserves. Her pickled pears were a revelation. The making of these was part of Carrington's secret life. I was in her confidence in all such occupations, for I shared her tastes, and it was I who had introduced her to Cobbett's *Cottage Economy*. Sometimes things went wrong. Her first attempt at bottling broad beans led to a series of explosions and to the most nauseating smell.

Ralph Partridge took over the vegetable garden, the greenhouse, the orchard and the bees. In all these pursuits they shared, and they became the chief bond between them. When Ralph went to live in London with Frances Marshall, Carrington felt betrayed by a partner in the vegetable garden bed as much as in the matrimonial. He did what he could to help in the garden during weekends for he loved Ham Spray. Between them they produced much of the food which they ate.

Much later during the Second World War Ralph carried the production of food even further, and Ham Spray retained much of its earlier flavour. Sometimes there were surprises of a startling sort. On one visit I was told not to use the best bathroom. It had a specially long bath, in which Lytton could lie at full length, and the walls were lined with tiles that Carrington had painted with shells and starfish and sea anemones before having them fired. I was to use the other bathroom down the passage. But I forgot the injunction, and on stepping into the best bathroom, I was appalled to see a corpse lying at full length, half submerged in the bath. For the tenth of a second I thought that a murder was being concealed. . . Who was the victim? Then I saw that the white skin was not human . . . the carcase of a large white pig was being cured in brine.

When I came for a weekend to Ham Spray with my wife, Ray, Carrington put us into the best bedroom with the very large four-poster bed—that which she had drawn with Lytton sleeping in the garden at Tidmarsh because it was too big to be taken into the house. In the morning Ralph would bring us early morning cups of tea.

Breakfast was lavish. Ham and eggs, kedgeree or kippers, coffee, a large bowl of fresh cream just skimmed from the pans of milk, hot rolls, butter, marmalade, damson cheese and honey in the comb. During the morning I would go for a walk with Lytton on the downs, while Ralph strayed about—in spring looking for plovers' eggs or in the autumn gathering mushrooms. Or else we were driven to some hidden Wiltshire village, or to one of Carrington's favourite spots. Then towards evening the games of bowls and after dinner sitting watching the parent barn owls ferrying mice from the stack-yard on an average of one every three minutes, to the owlets in the great beech.

At Ham Spray there was a continual stream of guests: Sebastian Sprott, Morgan Forster, Roger Senhouse, Eddie Sackville-West, Saxon Sydney-Turner, Rachel MacCarthy, Julia Strachey and Stephen Tomlin, Topsy Lucas, Dadie Rylands, Raymond Mortimer ... all lazily enjoying Lytton's conversation and *la douceur de vie* provided by Carrington.

Olive, the cowman's daughter, came in to help and Ralph enjoyed doing much of the heavy work. One result of his going to live with Frances Marshall in London, and only coming down for weekends, was that much more work fell on Carrington, who could seldom find time to paint or to construct her charming glass pictures, usually having tinsel or silver foil backgrounds. And then, in contrast to a house overflowing in summer, in winter, if Lytton were absent on a jaunt, she would be alone—riding Belle on the downs, cherishing her cats and writing letters.

Of course, she went on jaunts also—to France with Dorelia John and often to stay with her and Augustus at Fryern Court.

Her long love affair with Gerald Brenan is well documented, and I saw nothing of it. But she did invite me to be her companion at a party given by Beakus Penrose on his Brixham ketch, then tied up at Southampton. Topsy Lucas had come to look after Lytton while she was away. It was winter and very cold. Carrington drove over the downs and Salisbury Plain to Southampton. The deck of the boat was slippery with hoar frost, but all was warm and shipshape below—the long saloon gleaming with polished brass and mahogany. We drank—I expect it would be safe to say—rum punch, and black velvet (stout and champagne). At any rate there was no lack of liquor and of delicious food, and I think Carrington had a hand in cooking the dinner. And here I should like to contradict Michael Holroyd, who gives the impression that Carrington was a bad cook. I can do so safely as I ate her dishes and he did not. She became a very good cook in the style of the old-fashioned English inn.

When we went on deck after dinner it was to find that all was deep in snow. I was put to sleep in a cubby-hole where I nearly suffocated. Soon after dawn I scrambled ashore and went for a walk through the deep snow, seeing some flying-boats moored not far away. Everything was magical, and the icy air restored and excited me.

Carrington and I drove back through deep snow unmarked by a footprint or wheel mark over the downs and reached Ham Spray. I never felt closer to Carrington or more sure that she was fond of me, even though, *faute de mieux*, I was sometimes to console her as a lover when she was unhappy.

After I went to live at Hilton Hall in Huntingdonshire, I became interested in the contradictory character of Oliver Cromwell, who was born nearby, and on one of my visits to Ham Spray I told Lytton that he ought to write about him—a subject far better suited to his pen than that of Elizabeth and Essex. I told him that there was a Welsh streak in Cromwell (his paternal grandfather's name was Williams) and that he might find qualities in him in common with Lloyd George—but that unlike him Cromwell belonged to the new aristocracy.

Lytton tittered and withdrew from the proposal. It would mean years devoted to studying ridiculous sectarians—Fifth Monarchy men, Levellers, Presbyterians, Shakers, Quakers. No—it was impossible. The romantic streak in him made him prefer lace ruffles, velvet breeches and hats adorned with ostrich feathers to the shorn locks, plain white collars and severe doublets of the Roundheads. But Lytton was not Dumas. He would have done far better with a sympathetic study of the revolutionaries, spiced with their absurdities, than with the intrigues of the court, the struggle among aristocrats for power, the treacheries of their hangers-on.

We walked up and down the lawn and then up to the fruit garden where there was the pretence of a tennis court, I pleading my case to Lytton, who could see only the horrors involved: he would have to read all of Bunyan, sum up Milton and live with the Puritan divines. I urged the claims of silver-tongued Henry Smith, but it was impossible.

I gave up, thinking that perhaps if I had made the suggestion in

1919—at the time of the Peace Conference—the likeness between Cromwell and Lloyd George would have tempted him, and he would have reacted differently, but at that time I had known nothing of Cromwell and was not interested in his character.

I was in France during the long agony of Lytton's death from cancer of the stomach and perforation of the intestines. His last words, I have been told, spoken to his sister Pippa were: 'If this is death, I don't think much of it.'

On my return to England I stayed in a room over the Nonesuch Press offices when I was in London. Ralph Partridge and my sister-in-law Frances rented a flat on the floor above. They asked me if I would come with them and Carrington to Biddesden, to which they had been invited for the weekend by Bryan Guinness. Carrington had painted the largest of her glass pictures on a blind window there—a *trompe l'œil* of the cook looking out of the kitchen window, with a cat beside her. It is, I believe, the last of her paintings, and she was pleased with it. After our visit she wrote: 'The picture of the cook on the wall is perhaps the only picture I ever brought off. I am glad that Lytton saw it and liked it.'

I realised that Ralph thought my presence might make things easier during the visit and accepted. Carrington was quiet, self-possessed and pleased to see me there. Perhaps I was too careful not to speak of Lytton or of her future.

Just before we left she reminded Bryan that she had asked him to lend her one of his shotguns. Rabbits were overrunning the garden at Ham Spray, and she could easily shoot one out of her bedroom window.

The request was made in the presence of Ralph. Carrington had attempted to commit suicide while Lytton was dying, and I was surprised that Ralph did not try to stop Bryan lending the gun. The fact was that he had become exhausted by the strain of looking after her. So Carrington took the gun with her. Some weeks later, Ralph left her alone at Ham Spray. She shot herself, but did not kill herself. The gardener heard her groans, and she told him to telephone to Ralph and to summon a doctor.

I was woken up by Ralph who told me the news. Luckily I had my car in London, and I drove Ralph and Frances to Ham Spray as fast as I dared and as my car would go.

I did not go into the room while Carrington was dying, but after her death I went for an intolerable moment and looked at her. There was no sign in her features of the pain she must have suffered. It was the face of a proud woman.

George Moore

George Moore

'A bit of a goose and a bit of a genius,' was my grandfather Richard
Garnett's summing up of George Moore, a verdict which my mother
was fond of repeating. To her the genius was more apparent than the
goose, whose undeniable presence my father insisted on.

G.M. was born in Moore Hall, built at the end of the eighteenth
century looking out over the pellucid waters of Lough Carra in County
Mayo in Ireland. It was a large house, with plenty of stabling and out-
houses behind, approached by a private road winding through
woodland, and there was a long wooded peninsula beyond the house
jutting into the lake on the right-hand side.

The loveliness of the lake, the beauty of the position of the house, the
character of the peasantry, influenced Moore deeply and grew more and
more important to him as the years went on. When Moore Hall was
burned in 1923 it was a tragedy for him, and the imbecile act of
vandalism was only mitigated by the fact that he had brought away a
painting he greatly valued as a precautionary measure a few weeks
before.

During a civil war the ignorant and brutal come to the top, and
atrocities are committed on historic enemies. But the burning of Moore
Hall was particularly imbecile, as the Moores were an old Irish family.
G.M.'s father had been a Catholic and a Nationalist politician opposing
the Union, a natural leader of his countrymen.

G.M.'s first ambition was to be a gentleman jockey and to win
steeplechases. But jockeys are small men with light compact bodies. A
tall man with a long body, loosely put together, with sloping shoulders,
is physically handicapped. George Moore had very fair hair, very blue
eyes and, right into old age, the delicate complexion of a young girl.

An heir to an estate naturally looked for a bride with a fortune, and for
a little while G.M. haunted the Dublin marriage-market. He was a
young man with one of the rarest gifts; that of sympathetic understand-

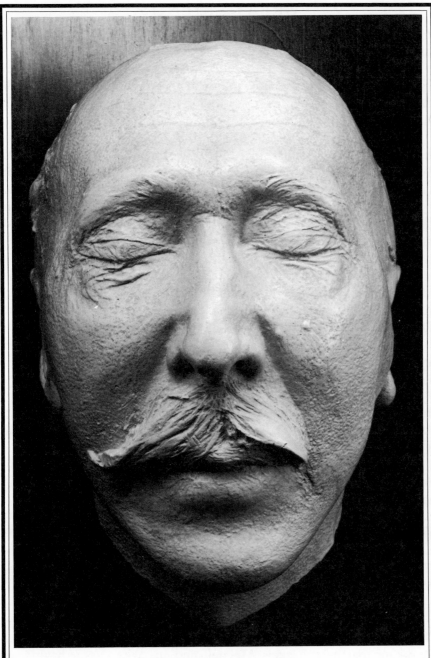

GEORGE MOORE
death mask in the National Portrait Gallery

ing, of being able to put himself in the shoes of a fellow-creature entirely unlike himself.

He watched the girls in the Dublin marriage-market who had been brought there to find husbands, and the helpless ignoble predicament of these young women inspired him to write his first novel, *A Drama in Muslin*.

But he had already abandoned his ambition as a jockey and decided to be a painter. Paris was the place for that, and he soon was sharing a studio with a friend in the Latin Quarter. It was, as was proper in those days, filled with hookahs, brass Arab lamps, curved daggers and oriental rugs thrown over ottomans—and on the easels were daubs of nautch girls in Turkish trousers with bare midriffs, dancing to castanets and tambourines.

Although he was no good as a painter, the young art student was able to haunt the cafés and to learn a certain amount of French and to scrape acquaintance with Manet and meet Turgenev and Zola. They opened his eyes; he threw over paint and turpentine for pen and ink and paper. The grimy realism of *L'Assommoir* replaced the nautch girls and castanets. Luckily for literature Moore, unlike Zola, was not a propagandist. His powers of sympathy and his feeling for the poetry of nature and in human existence were like those of Turgenev.

A Mummer's Wife and *Esther Waters* were the magnificent fruits of this conversion, which brought him fame among the discriminating, though his greatness as a novelist has never been really recognised—he is forgotten, and Hardy occupies his rightful place.

W. B. Yeats and the Celtic movement took him back to Ireland. He hated Catholicism, but his powers of sympathy and understanding enabled him to see into the heart of the priest who is the hero of *The Lake* and to write *A Letter to Rome*, a story of which Turgenev might have been proud. Ireland induces a sense of the absurd—not among its natives—but in the returning exile and visitor. G.M.'s three volumes *Hail and Farewell* reveal the absurd qualities of his friends, Yeats and Martyn in particular.

One day in 1924, when I went into the office of the Nonesuch Press I found my partners Francis Meynell and his wife, Vera, having an argument. They had just received a letter from G.M. He had been struck by the appearance of Nonesuch books and would like us to publish an essay he had written on the nature of poetry. It was to be called *Pure Poetry*, and to be followed by an anthology of the rare examples of Pure Poetry to be found in the English language.

Francis Meynell hated George Moore for family reasons. G.M. had been attracted by the poetry—and, I believe, by the person—of Alice Meynell before her marriage to that ardent Catholic, Wilfred Meynell, who ran the Catholic publishing house of Burns and Oates. And then Moore had written that Alice's gifts as a poet had been destroyed by her marriage and the Catholicism of her dull husband. I fancy that he may have been right about this. So Francis wanted nothing to do with the dastard who had insulted his parents. Vera, as usual, took a business view: George Moore's name would look well on our list. She admitted that she had read little if anything of his—but that was irrelevant.

I had read much of the best of G.M.'s work and felt a great admiration for him, so I sided with Vera, and we won the day—on condition that Francis should never have to speak to him and that I should be responsible for the negotiations. Nothing could have pleased me better, and soon afterwards I had lunch with G.M. in Ebury Street. Many lunches followed, and the menu was almost always the same: a whiting—a fish I despise, two tiny lamb cutlets, mashed potatoes, tinned peas. This was followed by Bird's Custard and tinned pears. With this, a small glass of hock for me. G.M. was abstemious and no gourmet.

The genteel and lifeless repast did not matter in the least: I would willingly have swallowed another helping of Bird's Custard in order to prolong my visit. G.M. was very gentle, very polite and beautiful for a man of sixty-one. He had a yellowish-white drooping moustache and the general shape of a long hock bottle dressed in rather new Irish tweeds. He was—unexpectedly—a natural aristocrat. His hands gave him away. Anyone with those hands would have been hurried to the guillotine at once.

His thesis on Pure Poetry was that only poetry which confines itself to things will endure. Ideas change so rapidly, but the poetry of nature is immortal. Thus God, general ideas and moralising are impurities, which it is essential to keep out. I asked G.M. if he had formed much of the anthology which was to illustrate his theme. I did not hint that a second anthology might be made to disprove it. I don't think such a disloyal notion had entered my head. What he said must be right.

Suddenly I realised with a shock that the goose was talking, not the genius.

'Mr Atkinson. . .' he said, 'Mr Atkinson. . .' Mr Atkinson was hard at work—he was coming to supper on Friday with the results of his labours. For Mr Atkinson was making the anthology. G.M. could not be expected to wade through the corpus of English poetry, he was not equipped to search for and find the examples that would prove his thesis. Mr Atkinson was the very man for it . . . and that reminded him that Mr Atkinson would have to be paid.

I was profoundly disturbed, but I had the heroism to tell him that Mr Atkinson's remuneration was something they must settle between themselves. Our offer was the whole book, published under his name— not for a work of collaboration.

Later I probed a little, and it became clear that G.M. could not remember a single poem which qualified.

'I feel sure that there is something in Poe . . . Baudelaire admired Poe.' I refrained from saying that I did not.

He came to the door with me and stood for some time watching me disappear up Ebury Street, his beautiful old face wreathed in smiles.

I did not tell my partners about Mr Atkinson and the large part that he would play. I said he had a secretary who was looking things up and copying them out, and that I had told G.M. that he would have to pay for all the research and secretarial work he thought necessary. So in due course Mr Atkinson coughed up the required amount of Pure Poetry, and the book was published. No doubt G.M. went through the collection and approved it.

I was asked to lunch soon afterwards, and my reception was most cordial. He had asked Mary Hutchinson about me and she had made him read my book *A Man in the Zoo*. He seldom read any of the younger writers (he was not a great reader), and I was fortunate enough to have pleased him. When he asked me what I was writing, I told him the subject of *The Sailor's Return*. This interested him, and he asked to read what I had already written. I sent the manuscript to him as I wrote it, and he wrote to me almost every other day about it. His first letters were most encouraging. But when he got to my ending, I received a severe rap over the knuckles. In my original version, my hero, a publican, becomes a professional prizefighter and is killed in a prizefight.

G.M. wrote that the story of the publican becoming a prizefighter and being killed might be a good story, but it was irrelevant to the subject of his bringing a black girl to live in an English village and the racial antagonism it aroused, and that I must scrap the ending. I pondered the subject for a morning and saw that he was right. I had spent days poring over the annals of prizefighting in *Boxiana*, studying the different styles and tricks of the great bare-fisted champions, and reading of the feud between the men from Brummagem and the East End—usually Jewish champions. Now I was told that all this had to be thrown away . . . I had switched to a different story, and the unity of my book had been destroyed.

But G.M. was right. I cut out the professional pugilism and wrote a new ending. Another criticism came. But it was from the goose, not the genius. I resisted it, for I knew that I was right. G.M. objected to my black heroine becoming a scullery maid in the inn after her husband's death. It was too sad. He wanted me to put her on board the ship that takes her young son back to Dahomey. That would have been to destroy the book, which is a tale of racial intolerance.

By that time G.M. and I had become friends, and I was a fairly frequent visitor to Ebury Street. I listened to the goose as well as to the great writer, and I wish I remembered more of their conversation. He was, or had been, a rather social figure. Virginia Woolf describes meeting him and a conversation they had in a wonderful letter to Vita Sackville-West.

Never did anyone talk such nonsense as George . . . but I can't tell you how urbane and sprightly the old poll parrot was and (this I think is what using the brain does for one) not a pocket, not a crevice, of pomp, humbug, respectability in him; he was as fresh as a daisy.

He could be amusing. My sister-in-law got wedged against him in a crowded cocktail party, and overheard him say: 'But I only kissed the brim of her hat.'

Which reminds me of the Irish lady who said: 'Some men kiss and tell. Other men kiss and don't tell. George Moore doesn't kiss and tells.'

That suggests that G.M. was a bit of a cad. I am inclined to believe that this is true of almost all great writers—or at all events the realists who take the whole of human life and experience as their subject. Some perfect gentlemen, who aspire to be realistic writers (I am thinking of John Galsworthy) turn their eyes away from some of the mean, bitchy, comic characteristics of men and women. But the great writer is like a child that has not been taught that some things must not be said, or even observed.

To give an example: If I were including among these sketches one of a certain beautiful and talented woman, I would, for the sake not only of truth, but to explain our subsequent relationship, record why I never became her lover. It was because the bed broke. It happened sixty years ago in the Berkeley Hotel after lunch. It was essential for my companion's reputation to disguise the accident, and I spent the hour I might have been in her arms in nailing the cheap and shoddy structure that the luxury hotel provided together again with the heel of my shoe. That might have happened to Galsworthy—Ada's reputation would have been jeopardised—but can one imagine his recording it? G.M. on the other hand would have extracted all the humour, all the anxiety, all the exasperation of a situation which had instantly—and strangely enough forever—abolished the lusts of the flesh.

Perhaps if one investigated the novels which G.M. excluded from the canon of his work, one would discover not only the writings of the goose—but also bits of the cad. A minor character in Stendhal's novel *Armance* says of the hero: '*Il est trop bien né pour écrire*' Luckily most of us have escaped that. But G.M., the goose, might have believed that he was.

Having established G.M. as a Nonesuch author, I learned a good deal about his methods of writing, besides hearing his contemptuous attacks on his rivals—Hardy in particular. *Pure Poetry* and *A Communication to my Friends* were both trifles, but *Ulick and Soracha* was a long historical novel, set in Norman Ireland. It caused me nearly as much suffering as any of my own books. It was a long and tedious story, but that would not have mattered had it been well written. After reading the first version, dictated to his secretary, Miss Kingdon, I did not conceal my opinion, and to my surprise G.M. agreed. When I drew his attention to the phrase, 'Soracha's possible violation by Scottish soldiery', he groaned and held up his hands in horror. He rewrote the book—'putting English upon it', as Yeats would have said. It was better, but G.M. was not satisfied, and he rewrote much of it again, and Miss Kingdon typed and retyped.

This turned out to be his method of work. The goose would dictate, and then the genius would polish and repolish—for he had an ear.

This was the opposite from Henry James, whose first version is powerful and natural, but who tried to fold in—as cooks say—more and more implications when he rewrote. If James had ever written, 'The cat sat on the mat', when he came to rewrite, he might have improved that statement thus: 'Not purring, but with what empathy she rested until the door should open and morsels from *le boucher chevaline* tempt her to rise. Until then she was immobile on—I was almost forgetting to say— the mat.' Miss Kingdon could never have written of G.M., 'the typewriter was a positive spur', as Miss Bosanquet wrote of her employer.

GEORGE MOORE

Ulick and Soracha, as published, is rather tedious, but it is full of beauty, and it is well written. G.M. was a slave to his first inspiration. I remember his saying, almost in despair: '*Ulick and Soracha* is full of woods, and I have got to make each wood different.' It was against his creed as an author to leave one or two of them out.

A greater difficulty was a large rock, which, for some reason, lay in the path that Ulick had to pursue. G.M. could have abolished the rock at a stroke of the pen, or Ulick could have walked round it. But such tricks were unthinkable.

'Hannibal melted a rock that barred the way for his army in the Alps with scalding vinegar. But there cannot have been much vinegar in Ireland in the twelfth century, and that would have been malt vinegar.'

He was in despair. To use malt vinegar would have been most distasteful. His salads were always dressed with the best wine vinegar. For Ulick to use malt vinegar offended him.

I suggested that the rock might be split by fire. The idea delighted him. The rock was in the middle of one of the many woods, so there would be no shortage of fuel. A glorious pyre would be built against the rock, and when it was red-hot buckets of water would be thrown on it, and it would split into fragments with a tremendous noise, leaving a passage for Ulick de Burgo.

The story is full of beautiful transitions—both in time and in space. The art of transition—of carrying the reader easily and almost unnoticeably across a period of months or years or from one country to another, is possessed by few novelists. I learned what I know of it by reading and re-reading *Ulick and Soracha*. G.M. was satisfied with the book except for the jacket. Francis Meynell had employed McKnight Kauffer to do a large design in red, printed on vegetable parchment. G.M. disliked the design. I objected to the parchment, which immediately began to crinkle and shrink, so that a quarter of an inch of the top and bottom of the binding was exposed, like the wrists of a schoolboy who has grown out of his clothes.

I had been acquainted with that beautiful young woman, Nancy Cunard, before I had met G.M. I then discovered that she loved him as though he were her father. He had been the lover of her mother, whom Nancy hated. Nancy's love for G.M. became a bond between us.* One day, on returning to my basement flat in 37 Gordon Square, I found an angry note from Nancy asking me where on earth I hid myself. She had

*The best portrait of Moore is her book *G.M.*, which all who appreciate him should read (Hart-Davis, 1956).

been all day looking for me. Did I not know that G.M. had just undergone a dangerous operation for prostate? He had enquired after me. Nobody visited him, and I was to go and see him at his nursing home at once.

I went the following afternoon, and as I walked up from Oxford Circus to Portland Place, the newspaper sellers were shouting: 'Result of the Grand National!'

G.M. was lying flat in bed, very wan and pale, and so feeble that he could only greet me with a smile and whispered politeness. However, he saw the evening paper in my hand asked sadly if there were any news. Nothing, he implied, could interest him.

'Tipperary Tim has won the National!'

Colour came into G.M.'s pale cheeks. He made an effort to sit up in bed. I pushed pillows behind his shoulders to support him.

'An Irish horse! I know exactly what his rider is feeling now! My greatest ambition was to win the Grand National. My father put up the same fences as at Aintree, but with no hard timber or rails, only brushwood, so that a horse should not break a leg. I have often ridden a clear course round those fences. Tipperary Tim! He must be a splendid Irish hunter—aged of course. Does it say how many years old? Or what races he has won before? And what is the name of his rider?'

My news had resuscitated G.M. He was a different man from the pale corpse-like figure lying flat on the bed when I had been shown in.

The sister, who came in to tell me that I was overstaying the time allotted, was astonished, particularly when G.M. ordered her to send out at once for a later edition of the newspaper, which would contain a full account of the race. When I left, I felt that the invalid was well on the way to recovery.

I never had the hardihood to ask Nancy whether G.M. was her father, but I persuaded myself that he was. Not only was she devoted, but there was a proprietary quality in her devotion as though he were her responsibility.

When I spoke of her to G.M. he turned the subject aside. I felt that it was not only that Nancy's hatred of her mother was painful and the fact that she was living with a Negro in Soho regrettable, but also that he was concealing something. The real evidence for his paternity was, I convinced myself, in their looks. Nancy had the same delicate complexion—like a white-heart cherry—as he had. But I wanted to believe that she was his daughter because I felt affection and admiration for both of them.

GEORGE MOORE

G.M.'s death in 1933 came as a shock, for I had not seen him for some months. I attended his cremation at Golders Green.

There were few mourners. Nancy was in France, and did not come over. Besides myself were Ramsay MacDonald, then Prime Minister, Miss Kingdon, the secretary, the cook and the housemaid, and a rather forlorn old man whom I remembered having seen winding the clocks in Ebury Street. There may have been one or two other inconspicuous figures as well.

G.M. had once explained to me that he had been admitted to the Anglican Church because it was only by becoming a Protestant that he could make sure that a Roman priest did not slip into the room where he lay dying and assert that he had made a death-bed repentance.

For that reason there was a service conducted by an elderly Irish Protestant, Canon Douglas. He was undeniably drunk and forgot the words of the funeral service. My memory of it is something like this: 'Ashes to ashes and dust to dust. Forgive us our trespasses . . . glorious resurrection . . . our daily bread in the life everlasting. . .'

Ramsay MacDonald and I stood in reverent silence until this was over, a button was pressed and the coffin jerked forward and passed through the door to commit our old friend's body to the furnace. It seemed an appropriate end for a great writer whose work has always been undervalued by critics and the general reader.

Arthur Waley

Arthur Waley

When Noel Olivier's sister, Brynhild, married Arthur Ewart (Hugh) Popham, a lot of their friends went to Paddington Station to see them off on their honeymoon. Brynhild was lovely, her brilliant eyes like rainwashed jewels, and red cheeks—she shone with happiness, a bewitching Aphrodite. She was dressed in a red madder handwoven tweed that suited her.

Hugh was tall, pale, reserved and his momentary smiles seemed to be *contre-cœur*. As so often, his anxiety was to exhibit no emotion. Perhaps he was embarrassed by the presence of so many friends.

Before they got into their reserved carriage and were whirled away to Devon or Cornwall, I noticed a figure standing in the background, apart. He seemed to be a spectator—not one of our noisy group. He was Schloss, a Cambridge friend of Hugh's, and like Hugh destined to spend a great part of his life in the Print Room of the British Museum.

His face and bearing impressed me. I had never seen him before. He was aloof, apart, aristocratic and Jewish, silent until spoken to. When I next saw him, at some party, I tried to talk to him, to ask some question. He replied briefly, in dry tones and turned his head away. He had politely made it plain that he was not interested in me, or anything I might say.

He was a friend of Francis Birrell, and when Frankie and I became intimate friends, I saw more of Arthur. When the war came, he and his brother Hubert changed their name from Schloss to that of their mother: the ancient Norman Jewish name of Waley—meaning a foreigner. Arthur told Frankie that the name Schloss had been adopted for the sake of expediency in trade. My first impression had been right: Arthur was by birth a Jewish aristocrat, Spanish Sephardic on one side and from a Jewish family domiciled for centuries in Britain on the other. Arthur was poles apart from the gross and pushing Jew of the marketplace. His face was refined, lean and rather brown. He had

ARTHUR WALEY
photograph by Cecil Beaton

deep-set eyes, an aquiline nose, salient cheekbones, a sensitive mouth, and always had an air of aloof inconspicuous elegance. I met him at first most often in Hugh Popham's house—first in Regent Square and then in Caroline Place, bordering the Foundling Hospital.

In 1916 Frankie gave me his copy of Arthur's first translation, *Chinese Poems*, privately printed by Lowe Bros, 157 High Holborn, a little brochure that I still possess. I was excited by this new field of poetry and soon showed the translations to my father, who as a result got to know Arthur and became a lifelong admirer, always ready to praise his work.   As far as I know Arthur never wrote any original poetry, but he was, in my opinion, a great poet. Edward's warm appreciation and my enthusiasm for his translations led to a much closer friendship between us than at first seemed likely.

Although Arthur lived round the corner from Gordon Square and afterwards in it, he was never a member of the Bloomsbury Group.

Lytton Strachey had taken a dislike to him at Cambridge and could see nothing good in his poetry. He declared that the translations were not grammatical and greatly inferior to Giles's versions, etc., etc. As this was patently untrue, I never lost an opportunity of telling Lytton that he was blind and prejudiced, which did not help to make him change his mind. I think there was some personal quarrel at the back of Lytton's dislike. Among the older 'Bloomsburies' only Duncan Grant appreciated his translations at their true worth. He was a friend whom Arthur asked to design the jacket for *Monkey*.

Clive, Vanessa and Virginia thought him a bore, and I cannot dispute the fact that like many men who live alone, he could be one.

One of my early memories of Arthur is being invited to tea in his room round the corner from Gordon Square. From the moment of my arrival until my departure, Arthur talked about Hrosvitha, without vouchsafing any explanation of who he or she was, or why he was interested in him or her. I was left to discover in the course of his discourse that she was a German nun who lived in Cologne during the middle ages and had written . . . I know not what. It did not occur to Arthur that a young student of biology might not have heard of her, or be interested in her if he had.

I think Arthur was the greatest scholar I have known—the only one to rank with him was Jane Harrison. But scholarship often made him a bore. If Lytton Strachey had wanted to talk about Hrosvitha, he would have made what he said amusing, and would have brought before one's eyes a remarkable woman, breaking the shackles of the cloister with a goosequill. It did not occur to Arthur to be entertaining. He gave one the facts without explanation, as unaware of his listener as a gramophone playing its record—given with a rather jerky delivery.

If I was interested, as I often was, his talk was something to remember, if one wasn't, he was a bore. If he was interested in what I said, his shyness, dryness and aloofness vanished. He asked questions quickly, one after another. If the answer was not clear to him, he repeated it in different words, and as understanding came, one was rewarded.

In the early days Arthur bicycled everywhere in London. Later, he took to roller-skating, and, Brenan says, would skate all the way from Bloomsbury to Chelsea and back. In spite of his rather frail figure he was an expert skier, and went every winter to Switzerland for winter sports. I often saw him playing tennis in the garden of Gordon Square.

In the early 1920s he became associated with Beryl de Zoëte. She resembled an artificial flower made of highly polished black and yellow plastic. A middle-aged woman when I first met her, age did not wither her. The luxuriant crop of black dyed hair cut in a fringe shone with the same brilliance, and her rather yellow skin showed no wrinkles, when last I saw her. She had discovered, introduced and translated the work of Italo Svevo, the friend of James Joyce in Trieste, and she had visited Bali and was an authority on Polynesian dancing. But in spite of her talents most of us fled from her, and in consequence we saw less of Arthur than we otherwise should have done. Thus Beryl reinforced the Strachey hostility and helped to isolate Arthur from his Bloomsbury neighbours. Gerald Brenan and Francis Birrell were exceptions and saw much of Beryl. I never felt at ease in her company and could not think of the next sentence. Yet I felt sure that she was an intelligent and interesting woman. It did not help that in Beryl's eyes I was a creature of coarser clay—a bit of earthenware and she a cup of Meredithian porcelain. Arthur occasionally asked me to tea, and then I met Beryl. But the obstruction remained.

The last of my visits to Arthur's room in Gordon Square was macabre. My daughter, aged, I think, about fifteen, had read *Monkey* and had a passionate desire to meet Arthur. I wrote, and we were asked to tea. No one answered the bell, and, as the front door was unbolted, we pushed it open and went up to the room in which Arthur lived on the second floor. The door of his room was ajar, and, after knocking and getting no reply, we went in. I thought that Arthur might have remembered at the last minute that a young girl was coming to tea, and had rushed out to buy some sweet cakes, so it was reasonable to wait for his return. Arthur lived in the back room with a window looking out at the backs of the houses in Tavistock Square. The room was littered with objects, so that there was not room to put down one's hat. But unlike my own room, they were not scattered higgledy-piggledy, but each occupied its rightful place.

At one end of a table near the fireplace there were books and papers, at the other teacups laid out. Beyond there were cooking things ranged round a gas stove, with tins of food, and at the end where it would catch the light from the window, a narrow bench with a metal last sticking up, cobbler's tools, waxed thread and scraps of leather. Strange to say, Arthur mended his own shoes. He cooked his food, ate it, translated his books and mended his shoes in one room. I do not remember seeing a bed, but it is not impossible that there was one. This mode of existence was his choice, for Arthur cannot ever have been a poor man.

Henrietta and I had been inspecting the room for perhaps twenty minutes—we began to think that Arthur had forgotten that he had asked us to tea—when we heard a bloodcurdling scream come from the floor above . . . The screams were repeated. Someone was being murdered upstairs.

I ran up half the flight, calling out as I did so, but before I reached the top, a stalwart woman in nurse's uniform appeared. She told me that Miss de Zoëte was having one of her bad attacks, and that Mr Waley had run out to try and find the doctor.

Henrietta and I took our departure.

Not long afterwards Beryl died, and Arthur went to live in Switzerland.

At one of the birthday parties which I gave in the fifties, or early sixties, Arthur sent me as a present several pages of a manuscript which he had translated from the Chinese about a Buddhist hermit. On another birthday he came to the party which was given at Mariott Lefèvre's studio in London. My daughters were thus able to meet the translator of Murasaki's *The Tale of Genji* in its several volumes which they so much admired.

The last time I wrote to Arthur was after my stay in Southern Illinois where my friend Professor Lindegren had given me a magnificent Japanese painting of a wounded snake on a long scroll.* At one side there was an inscription which I asked Arthur to translate. I copied it out as exactly as I could and sent it him.

*The scroll can be seen in the background of the photograph reproduced here as frontispiece.

ARTHUR WALEY

I had moved on to the University of California, Davis, when I got Arthur's reply:

Nov 17th [1964]

Dear Bunny, It says: Dai'en, senior monk of the Koyasan, and on the right a kind of rebus made out of stylised Sanskrit characters which I cannot read. I am very well and do occasionally translate a Chinese poem; but in the main I read about Victorian writers. I am living at Highgate. Yours Arthur.

Some years later, when I was living in the houseboat *Moby Dick*, opposite Cheyne Walk, Gerald Brenan rang me up to say that Arthur was dying, and that he would like a visit from me. I rang up and arranged to go to see Arthur next morning. But he had died in the night.

H. G. Wells

H. G. Wells

Three men came out of the wood and walked up the garden path by the apple trees. On one side the tall figure of Edward, on the other that of Sydney Olivier, tall, dignified and bearded. Between them a chubby figure bounded along, looking like a small boy being guarded by two policemen. As regards Olivier that may not have been far from the truth. It was H. G. Wells, bouncing like a rubber ball between the two tall striding men. He was staying with Olivier, as he had formed a plan of taking the Fabian Society out of the hands of Mrs and Mr Sidney Webb. Olivier was a leading Fabian and wanted to hear what Wells had to say.

Before the crucial election Edward joined the society simply in order to vote for Wells. Though she disliked Mrs Sidney Webb and her brand of bureaucratic Socialism, Constance was indignant because Edward was not a Socialist, only 'spoiling for a fight', and liked Wells.

On another occasion the four Olivier girls brought Wells round. I remember his response to Brynhild's sparkling eyes and flashing smile. But any attraction they felt for each other was suppressed, and its expression averted, as we played a violent game of rounders after tea.

Wells by then was a rising novelist and lived at Sandgate, where his literary neighbours were Henry James, Conrad and Ford. Then, when he published *Ann Veronica*, all hell broke loose. A brilliant young woman from Girton decided to have a child by Wells. Instead of keeping quiet, her parents denounced Wells to everyone. H.G. was thrown out of his club—the Savile—and was cut by conventional society. His crime had been greatly increased because *Ann Veronica* had been based on the affair. At one time Wells had seemed a possible recruit for the Tories, but after *Ann Veronica* that was forever impossible. It is often good for the character to be made a social outcast for a little while. Wells left Sandgate and bought a lovely old brick house in Church Row, Hampstead.

The scandal ran its course. Its heroine covered her scarlet sin with a

H. G. WELLS
painting by Pamela de Bayou

double coat of whitewash by marriage to Mr Blanco White, descendant of that learned pillar of Protestantism, the Spanish priest who after abjuring Popery and settling in England, added to his name of Blanco the English White.

Olivier though remaining friendly with Wells, wrote to say he would prefer him not to be seen in public in the company of his daughters. Lady Olivier, less moderate, forbade them to read Wells's *The Sea Lady*, a prohibition which was not observed after they borrowed Edward's copy of the book.

Olivier's letter was the cause of a strange scene. At the very height of the scandal, I went one day with Brynhild Olivier to a picture gallery in Bond Street. Brynhild suddenly caught sight of H.G., who was hiding from us behind some pictures on a stand in the centre of the room. She called out to him in her clear voice, and H.G. turned and bolted like a rabbit. But he took refuge in a cul-de-sac where Brynhild and I ran him to earth. Brynhild's cheeks were scarlet as she held out her hand, and her eyes flashed more than ever as she said: 'I won't let you cut me Mr Wells. So don't ever dare to try to do it again.'

I don't think I ever saw her look more lovely than she did at that moment. She held H.G. in talk for some minutes and forced him to look at some of the pictures with us. I could see that he was pleased, and at the same time uncomfortable and wanting to get away.

Edward and Constance would have seen very much less of H.G. if it had not been for his social eclipse and his move to Hampstead. For a time he lost many of his Socialist friends, who were afraid of the label of 'Free Love' getting attached to the movement. I always thought that was getting the priorities wrong. So I think did my mother's great friend, Dollie Radford.

It was probably a few years later that she wrote a play one performance of which was produced at the Little Theatre. I and most of the audience found it terribly embarrassing: a bad and sentimental version of her own life. 'What on earth can one say to Dollie?' was the thought in all her friends' minds. But H.G. was there to save the situation.

'Come along, all of you. I have booked tables. . .' And in no time at all we were all drinking champagne, and any doubts that Dollie may have had about the success of the evening were forgotten.

While he was at Sandgate H.G. had written *Little Wars*, a treatise on the tactics of playing with toy soldiers when armed with a miniature fieldgun, which could shoot wooden shells a distance of five or six yards.

BRYNHILD OLIVIER

Once when Constance was having tea with Jane Wells, H.G. took me
into the basement, where a room was devoted to the game. His sons
Frank and Gyp, both a good deal younger than me, were engaged in a
mimic battle, but H.G. sent them off unceremoniously to have their tea,

while we took their places lying on the floor and exchanging a few shots at each other's men.

A schoolboy does not get invited to lunch or dinner, so that it was not until some years later, after I had started work as a student at the Imperial College of Science, that I saw H.G. again. He stopped me in the street. 'I hear that you are following in my footsteps,' he said, for he had been a student there. I grinned in reply.

It was in the College magazine, the *Phoenix*, that the first version of *The Time Machine* appeared in print. While I was there one of the editors found and appropriated the manuscript from which it was printed.

It was while I was a student, that H.G. gave a fancy-dress ball to which I was invited. I wore a dress of white satin and danced with Countess Von Arnim (*Elizabeth in her German Garden*) and was introduced to Henry James. The small hall was crowded with celebrities, so the *Ann Veronica* scandal must have been well on the way to being forgotten—though it was soon to be followed by others.

I read Wells assiduously, and liked particularly *Tono-Bungay*, which came out as a serial in Ford's *English Review*. The war came, and Wells was one of the writers employed in the Ministry of Information after its creation in 1916. He was a bellicose patriot and wrote of 'The War to End War'. Neither he, nor anyone until Keynes, foresaw that it would be followed by 'A Peace to End Peace'.

I did not see him then for several years, but in 1922 I fulfilled his prophecy of following in his footsteps, by abandoning science for authorship. And a month or so after my first book was published H.G. reviewed it in the *Adelphi*. His words gave me more pleasure than any review of my books.

'I have nothing to say about how it is done, because I think it is perfectly done and could not have been done in any other way.' And he went on to compare it to a kitten—a thing with life of its own. It will be thought ungrateful if I cannot return the compliment. Most of H.G.'s work is imperfectly done. What he says of it himself is all too true: 'much of my work has been slovenly, haggard and irritated; much of it hurried and inadequately revised and some of it as white and pasty as a starchfed nun.'

But that apology shows his gift for *le mot juste*.

I did not see him for a few years after that review, though he sent me friendly messages through his secretary, Marjorie Craig, whom I met at parties given by Francis and Vera Meynell. Then he invited me down to

H. G. WELLS

Easton Glebe, his house on Lady Warwick's estate. My most vivid memory of that visit is playing a game which H.G. had invented. It was rather like badminton, played with the bare hand and a bouncy rubber ball and in a barn. H.G. was nearly twice the age of the three young people playing with him, but he left us all breathless and exhausted. The ball bounced, and so did H.G. He was always in the right place either to return the ball or pass it to his partner.

H.G. had always shown me the greatest kindness, but it was not until 1936 that we became real friends, as a result of this letter.

> 13 Hanover Terrace, Regent's Park, N.W.1
> Nov. 3 1936

Dear David,

I have taken to writing rather long short stories again and find I do not know quite what to do about publishing them.

I'd like to talk it over with you.

Yours ever,

> H.G.

Not that you are a publisher but I think you know about these things.

I lunched with H.G. soon after receiving his letter and was given the manuscript of *The Croquet Player* and asked if I might show it to a close friend of mine, Charles Prentice, who was then the senior partner of Chatto and Windus. A day or two later I had tea with H.G. who told me he had accepted Chatto's offer. They got the little book out in just over three weeks to publish in time for the Christmas sales.

It was a very remarkable achievement.

H.G. sent me a copy inscribed,

> David
> from H. Goliath Wells

Not many people seem to have read *The Croquet Player*. Like H.G.'s prophecies of Flying Machines, War in the Air, Tanks, Splitting the Atom and Going to the Moon, it is truer now than when it was written. The little story was inspired by H.G.'s realisation, before most people in England, of what was going on in Germany under Hitler. The hero is an inoffensive escapist who hears the story of a doctor who, after buying a practice in the Fens, became aware of an endemic evil in the countryside, an inheritance from cave man.

... he was shut off from us and hidden. And now we see him here face to face and his grin derides us. Man is still what he was. Invincibly bestial, envious, malicious, greedy. Man, sir, unmasked and disillusioned, is still the same fearing, snarling, fighting beast he was a hundred thousand years ago. . . Civilization, progress, all *that*, we are discovering, was a delusion. . . It is breaking down all about us and we seem unable to prevent it.

That was written forty-two years ago. We have only to turn the knob of the radio to hear that the most terrible of H.G.'s prophecies is coming true.

In the palmy days of the Nonesuch Press I could always find a bed above the Great James Street office. But in 1936 I had been reduced to taking a room in the National Hotel when I stayed for a night in London. H.G. found this out and told me that I could stay at 'Mr Mumford's' when it suited me and Siegfried Sassoon wasn't in occupation. The splendid houses in Hanover Terrace have each a garden, and at the end of H.G.'s garden was what had been the stables and coachman's house with its entry in Hanover Terrace Mews. H.G. put this coachman's house into good repair and called it 'Mr Mumford's' after an imaginary character of his invention.

It was delightful. I was given a key and could go and come as I pleased. Sometimes when I rang up to ask whether Mr Mumford's was free, H.G. would invite me to dinner. But he always liked me to come to breakfast. So in the morning, instead of slinking off into the Mews, I would walk up the garden, past the statue of Voltaire, and have breakfast, at which meal H.G. was always lively and amusing. When I had dinner, it was often *à trois* with Moura Budberg with whom I formed a friendship which lasted till her death. She brought a warmth which made H.G. happy and made me feel an accepted intimate. We joined in a conspiracy to keep H.G. cheerful, for his thoughts ran on the future of mankind and had become increasingly grim.

He asked me to bring my wife, Angelica, to dinner and was astonished that Clive Bell, whom he disliked, should have had such a beautiful daughter. I was unable then to reveal the well-kept secret that her father was Duncan Grant.

It is very difficult to give an idea of an amusing talker's conversation—at least I find it so.

I remember two references to the lady who was the original of Dolores in that very funny book *Apropos of Dolores*.

He named her, but I could not remember at the moment who she was.

'Oh, you know,' said H.G. rather petulantly, 'the woman I wronged.'

H.G. had once invited Lord and Lady Grenfell to dinner, and 'Dolores' was the fourth.

'And what is your chief occupation and interest in life?' Lady Grenfell asked, in what Dolores thought was in insufferably condescending manner.

'Fucking,' she replied in her heavy foreign accent.

H.G. was always irresistibly funny when describing his social embarrassments, of which the above is an extreme example.

To have been liked personally and to have had my work appreciated by this explosive genius is something I look back to with gratitude. But, apart from the personal element, I have always admired his blend of scientific intelligence and imagination. Understanding scientific thought, he could anticipate the impact on the world that its discoveries would bring. His scientific training also enabled him to scrub out his mistakes and start again from scratch. In that I think he was unique among the great men whom I have known.

If he had been a commanding public speaker with a deep voice, instead of one which rose to an indignant squeak, perhaps he might have saved England from the paper bureaucracy of the Webbs' Welfare State. But that is an idle speculation, for the churchmen, the hypocrites, the dullards and his own impatience would have got him down. And without that indignant squeak, would he have been H.G.?

His last days were haunted by the conviction that man would exterminate the human race. Prometheus had followed his gift of fire with that of the thunderbolts of Zeus, and had handed them to that 'envious, malicious, greedy . . . fearing, snarling, fighting beast' man. 'Civilization . . . is breaking down all about us and we seem unable to prevent it.'

T. E. Shaw

T. E. Shaw

Edward knew Colonel Lawrence of Arabia, who entrusted him with the abridgement of *The Seven Pillars of Wisdom* from the first Linotype edition of that book, printed at Oxford. He rejected Edward's abridgement after he was turned out of the Air Force because he wanted *Revolt in the Desert* to be a 'book for boy scouts'. Edward had chosen the most revealing passages, and then circumstances arose which made Lawrence want to hide himself. He gave Edward the copy of the Oxford Edition that he had worked on in gratitude for useless labour. He trusted him, saw him fairly often and corresponded a lot. Edward used to read aloud the letters of 'Little Imp', as he always called him. He and I corresponded too. Of course, I had read *The Seven Pillars*, with great excitement—preferring the Oxford Edition to the big illustrated privately printed quarto—of which I later owned a copy. Edward had subscribed for one, and Little Imp presented him with another. When Edward suggested sending it back, since no one could be entitled to two, he told him to give it to his son. I wrote to him about *The Mint*, his book on his experience as a recruit in the Royal Air Force, a letter which seems to have puzzled him. I thought the early part was like the record of some trapped animal. I wrote that *Seven Pillars* was 'a *Triumph*. . . . This an *Agony*'. He replied, 'You have put it in one word.'

He sent me great praise for my novel, *No Love*:

The Admiral was best of all. It was a most vivid study of several admirals I have known. The scene in the bakery, where he comes in and reads a poem, for which faculty nothing in anything you had said had prepared us, is altogether admirable. It struck me like a ballet. There was something so deliberate in the orchestration and arrangement, and the balance of art and life most beautifully kept.

And so on for three pages of appreciative criticism.

Two months later he wrote to Jim Ede whose life of Gaudier-Brzeska,

T. E. SHAW
photograph by R. G. Sims

Savage Messiah, I had just rejected for publication by the Nonesuch Press, and who was angry about it and wrote two letters to Shaw.

'One [letter] holds an admirable summation and demolition of the thesis of *No Love*! I am entirely with you. Such titillations of the spirit are prostitution, and nasty Maddox St. Prostitution at that. Better be like a bull and a cow in a field.' Later in his letter he tells Ede not to worry about David Garnett's criticism.

'The man is over-educated, too good a craftsman and so short-sighted . . . Your Gaudier is the goods.'

Incidentally I had rejected *Savage Messiah* because I thought it gave a false impression of a great artist whom I had known slightly, but whom neither Ede nor Shaw had ever met. 'Maddox St. Prostitution' is, I think, a reference to the Dorothy Warren gallery where D. H. Lawrence's 'obscene' paintings were seized by the police on the orders of the Home Secretary, Joynson-Hicks, and not to the professional ladies who lived in that street.

Shaw's letter was written to cheer up Ede, but I do not think it was dishonest. Ede's demolition was no doubt wholly convincing. Shaw's opinions on art and literature fluctuated and were uncertain. On reading my book, he wrote that I was a symbolist and 'every now and then one halts and says to oneself "This is supremely important: this *matters*".' Two months later it did not.

I first met Aircraftsman Shaw in 1929, after he had been sent back from India owing to a rumour that 'The Arch-Spy of the World' was assisting rebels in Afghanistan, and as some Labour Members of Parliament were ready to believe any nonsense, he had been flown home. I was working one evening at the office of the Nonesuch Press in Great James Street. Francis and Vera Meynell were out and I was alone in the house. The bell rang and there on the doorstep was Aircraftsman Shaw. He came in, but I felt uneasy lest Francis and Vera should return. So we went out and walked to my room in the basement of 37 Gordon Square.

My room in the basement had a narrow kitchen and bathroom projecting along one side of the area, facing the basement steps. For some reason—probably I was making coffee—we went into this room, and while I stood by the gas cooker, Shaw sat opposite me on the edge of the bath and we stayed there eagerly talking, long after we might have gone back into my room and sat down comfortably.

I told him that I intended to write the story of a long-distance flight, and he doubted if I could do it convincingly.

T. E. SHAW

I asked him about the translation of the *Odyssey*, which had occupied his hours off-duty at Miranshah Fort on the North-West Frontier. I asked him whether he had read Samuel Butler's *The Authoress of the Odyssey*, but he had not. I have always found his evidence very convincing, and we discussed the Author's curious ignorance of masculine affairs, handling boats, etc.

It may have been this conversation that led him to describe me as 'over-educated'—an absurd statement as I was hardly educated at all.

I asked Shaw what he was going to call his translation. An impish expression came on his face, and he replied:

'I have thought of calling it Chapman's Homer.'

I could not see the point of this joke, as I did not know that Shaw was an illegitimate son of Sir Robert Chapman, Bart. I asked him to explain.

'I am descended from Chapman. Mine is the second translation of the Odyssey to be made by one of the family,' is what he said. But it did not explain why he thought he had made a good joke. A man who was embarrassed by his illegitimacy would not have made it. And the fact that he had to conceal the truth while his mother and his elder brother were alive made trying to explain funnier still. Bob was a medical missionary in China. What a scandal if the facts had come out! And what a saving of dissimulation and agony if it had!

I think that the next time we met was when he dropped in at Hilton Hall—my old farmhouse in Huntingdonshire. But it has left no memory except watching the thickset little aircraftsman straddle his huge motorbicycle and go off with a roar to the crossroads.

Dozens of legends sprang up about that little man, and it is sometimes difficult to separate legend from truth. It is currently believed at Hilton that Shaw rode his motor-bicycle into the pond at the crossroads. Actually the man who had that misfortune was my friend, Geoffrey Webb.

Robert Graves and others have recorded that Shaw hated to touch, or to be touched by, another human being. And also, because of that, he would never fight hand to hand. There are however records of his wrestling, and a neighbour of mine at Hilton, Hugh Leycester, told me rather ruefully of his only contact with Aircraftsman Shaw. Before he came to live in the country and became a farmer, Hugh had had thoughts of becoming a publisher. He had gone into the firm of Jonathan Cape as sort of apprentice. *Revolt in the Desert* had been planned to help pay for the big *Seven Pillars of Wisdom*.

One day Shaw rode up to Cape's office, then in Gower Street, and soon afterwards came charging down the stairs, while Jonathan on the landing outside his room called out: 'Stop him! Stop him!' Hugh ran after Shaw into the street and caught hold of the handlebar of the motor-bicycle before Shaw had started it. Next moment he had been sent flying by a punch on the jaw and was lying against the railings beside the pavement. When Hugh had picked himself up, Shaw was half-way to University College. He was not exaggerating when he said that he was 'a pocket Hercules'.

In 1931, I published *The Grasshoppers Come*, which was the story of the long-distance flight of which I had spoken. Shaw wrote:

The book has pleased me quite beyond what I had thought possible. It is the first account of real flying by a real writer who can really fly: and it gave me a very great sense of long distance, and of that incommunicable cradle-dandling which is a cockpit in flight.

Two years later I had become Literary Editor of the *New Statesman*. It was before the paper moved to its present offices in Great Turnstile, and we had the top half of an old house next door to the pub, in Great Queen Street. I had a dingy room stacked with the manuscripts of poems and short stories which my predecessor had not had the cruelty to reject or the folly to publish.

I was wading through the accumulation when Shaw came in unannounced. He was very angry—and angry with me. He had just seen a copy of *The Legion Book* published to swell charities for the armed forces, and among its miscellaneous contents was the last chapter of *The Mint*, published without his knowlege or permission. Among its other contents was my story *Colonel Beech's Bear*.

Shaw had given Edward *The Mint*, copied out in small handwriting in a small quarto, which he had bound in Air Force blue niger. He had informed Edward that he had taken the original manuscript out into an airfield and burned it, and that the little volume was the only copy in existence.

Accompanying the gift were instructions that it was to be lent to a whole series of persons ranging from Air Chief-Marshal Sir Hugh Trenchard to John Buchan and E. M. Forster. As I thought there was a chance that one of these distinguished persons might steal it, or lose it in the post, I persuaded Edward to let my secretary at the Nonesuch Press, Marion Coates, type three copies while she was staying at Hilton Hall. Shaw knew this, and it was natural for him to jump to the conclusion that I had supplied the last chapter of *The Mint* to the Editor of *The Legion Book*, with whom I had been in contact.

He came in and looked at me with his eyes blazing, a man completely transformed by an internal force. For a few moments we stared into each other's eyes. My astonishment must have shown him at once that I was innocent, and I assured him that Marion was not only absolutely trustworthy, but also that she had not had the opportunity to steal any part of the book, and that the typescripts had never left Hilton Hall.

How then, I asked, in my turn, could *The Legion Book* Editor have got hold of *The Mint*? One of those to whom the book had been lent on Shaw's instructions, must be the guilty party.

Shaw had become his normal self again. He had seen that I was innocent and indeed incapable of such a breach of confidence. But my question embarrassed him. Only after his death did I discover that the story that he had taken the original manuscript out in Karachi and burned it, was untrue. He had kept it and given it to Bernard Shaw's wife Charlotte.

He said something unconvincing: it must have been a copy made by an officer in the R.A.F. to whom he had shown it. This officer must have given it to the Editor of *The Legion Book*. When Shaw left my office he was convinced that I had told the truth, the whole truth and nothing but the truth. But I was doubtful whether he had. There was no reason why he should. Once I had shown myself to be innocent, the facts, though interesting, did not concern me. I have wondered since if the criminal could have been Charlotte, or G.B.S.? They alone were in a position to do it.

It could not have been Air Chief-Marshal Sir Hugh Trenchard. That officer needed spectacles for reading. He must have mislaid them while *The Mint* was on loan to him, for he invariably referred to it as *The Unit*!

In my letter to Shaw after reading *The Mint*, I had teased him because he wrote of flying as 'The Freedom of the Air'. My comment was 'It is only a new form of transport.' This riled him, as I had hoped it would. Then I learned to fly an aeroplane myself and became as enthusiastic as he was. After the publication of my historical novel *Pocahontas* I was able to go shares with Jamie Hamilton in buying a small German Klemm aeroplane dirt cheap.

We kept it at Cambridge, and I invited Shaw to ride up from Southampton and fly with me. I did not know that he had been forbidden to fly by some fool in the Air Ministry. That may have been the reason that he countered my invitation by suggesting that I fly down to Eastleigh—the nearest airfield to Southampton—and that he would take me out in one of the high-speed launches which he had been designing with Scott-Paine.

Edward had a caravan at Hinckley and lent it for a weekend. I, my wife and two small sons drove there, and I flew over and landed on a piece of burned common ground near one of the Frensham ponds.

I had forgotten to bring a picket rope, but there was no gale that night and *Pocahontas*, as I called her, came to no harm.

Next morning I flew into Eastleigh, took a bus and met Shaw as arranged, at his lodgings in Birmingham Street.

He came out. It was the first time I had seen him not in uniform, and in the looser clothes the burly muscles were disguised. He asked me if I knew Southampton—and immediately we got stuck, for he proceeded to take me round and show it me. I had come to see him—not Southampton—but he had turned himself into a pedantic guide, speaking very precisely about what interested me not at all. He was something between a scoutmaster or a curate and an Oxford don, rather shy and celibate. I walked around with him making feeble assenting noises.

At last he led me to a ferry—I don't know which one—and when we got off we walked a short distance to The British Power Boat's yard. It was 10 June, and I think a Saturday. Anyhow the buildings were empty and unguarded.

We got into one of the launches. I think she was type No. 200. Shaw started the engines and we nosed up and I cast off the moorings. The clerical scoutmaster had vanished, and an entirely different human being—an eager, confident, weather-beaten mechanic—had slipped into his skin. We started away down Southampton Water. But when he opened up, he was not satisfied. The engine was not doing its revs.

'Take the helm and keep her in the centre of the fairway.' Then, leaving me in charge, with the engine ticking over, he went down the hatchway, ripped out a floorboard and stood on his head. When I looked down I could see a lock of his fair hair almost in the oil.

We slid along slowly, down the centre of the channel. I could not remember the rules, but decided to keep a straight course unless it was a sailing boat that crossed our path. Shaw stayed like a duck, upside down, groping in the engine for quite a while. Then he came up red-faced, happy, with his bare arms covered in grease, which he wiped off on a bit of cotton waste. He had tightened a gland, I think he said. He took over the controls, and suddenly we flew—yes flew, down Southampton Water.

T. E. SHAW

He was eager, excited, happy; as we simply roared over the water we looked at each other with joy. We had become happy, eager, accomplices because of the flying spray, made unselfconscious by the boat in her headlong rush. I saw then how wise he had been to go into the ranks of the R.A.F., with men on a job he liked. By that time he was working, on his own terms, more as a speedboat designer than simple mechanic. The high-ranking officers had learned at last to accept him and let him put himself to good use. Shaw's last commanding officer allows me to quote from his recollections:

I think King's Regulations at the time, they certainly expressed it so later on, specified that no one was allowed to coxswain boats unless he had either a First or Second Class coxwain's certificate, or superior qualification. But Shaw totally without such qualifications drove all manner of service boats. At the material time at Bridlington he'd completed an incredible number of tests on these boats including the epic trip of Seaplane Tender 200, the first of her class, which he took non stop, and single handed from Hamble to Plymouth; his log book is still in existence somewhere in M.O.D. . . . His status was that of the lowest grade of all—an aircraft hand, but everyone from Air Ministry to Catfoss, and indeed my coxswains and fitters in the unit, looked upon him as some very superior being, not only in the technical sense, but on account of his apparent flair for short circuiting all conventions and channels to secure his objectives.

When Shaw had shown me the boat's paces, he handed over the controls, and I took her back to the British Power Boat yard. After picking up our moorings, we stayed for some little while on board while Shaw showed me some of her points.

'The Navy,' he may have said, 'has too many men on board their ships, so they invent work for them to do. That is degrading. They make the fittings of brass because it needs a lot of polishing. I have put' (or it may have been 'we have put') 'stainless metal—it looks like brass. They have expensive teak decks that need constant holystoning. We have put a surface that only wants swabbing down with a mop and a bucket of water to keep it clean.'

And he explained—only I have forgotten—how the whole design and construction differed from a clinker-built boat with a keel. At top speed she lifted her bows, skimmed the waves and was partly airborne.

We went ashore, and, before we left the yard, I told Shaw that I wanted a picketing-rope for my aeroplane. We hunted round the deserted works to find one. Stray ropes had been tidied away, and Shaw scrupled to take one actually in use. At last a length was found, and we went on to take the ferry back to Southampton. On board were two North-Country young aircraftsmen. Shaw turned his back on me and began talking to them, telling them that two boats were being sent up to Scotland soon and there would be a chance for them to be part of the crews. They were excited and eager, breathless with gratitude. Quite suddenly Shaw turned to me, took the rope out of my hands and asked one of the men to splice an eye at one end, and the other to work a backsplice at the other. They set busily to work with their fingers and the spikes on their knives. By the time we reached Southampton the job was finished.

'They like being asked to do something,' said Shaw. It was obvious that they did. As I very much liked the beautifully finished off picket-rope, it was a magical arrangement.

They obviously knew who he was, and there was no itchy pretence that they did not on the part of Shaw. It had been different at the beginning. Morgan Forster told me how he had visited Shaw—or perhaps he was then Ross—at Bovington Camp, after he had enlisted in the Tank Corps.

They had gone into the canteen, and Shaw had assured him that his identity was unknown to all the men there. It was quite obvious to Morgan that this was untrue, and he became embarrassed because Shaw began showing off while keeping up the pretence. Air Commodore Manning shows that such behaviour was a thing of the past.

The airmen . . . resolved it quite simply; they accepted him as an airman. They knew about 'Lawrence of Arabia', but they associated it with a form of Beau Geste escapade; and they awarded no special points for that kind of thing. They were more concerned with the immediate Shaw and his capabilities in handling motor boats; and also whether he was gritty or co-operative. Their opinion seemed to be that he did pull his weight, had commendable technical qualities, and he was companionable, even if he wasn't startlingly hilarious. There was of course a gap of a generation between Shaw and all my airmen. He should have qualified for the usual nickname of 'Grandad' or 'Pop'.

This change was because in the Marine Craft Section he felt at home. He had hated being in the Tanks. Manning records Shaw's behaviour on occasions when they met socially, chuckling to himself at a play.

He sat right in the middle of us all, again wearing the scarf and the sports jacket. The wives of Ian Deheer and Weblin were there, and he was extremely sociable with them; he always seemed to be very much at ease in ladies' company. I remember him autographing their programmes and behaving in an almost juvenile way in the vestibule at the interval; in great form, nothing to suggest he resented woman's company. What impressed me on these isolated social occasions was his extraordinary normality in personal relationships, rather than abnormality, with people in all walks and conditions of life.

Shaw made several friends—lifelong friends—both in the Tank Corps and in the R.A.F. Many of his letters to them are included in the volume that I edited.

The only one of them I got to know well—he was a frequent visitor to Hilton Hall—was 'Jock' Chambers. His wife, Athene, came occasionally and painted in Ray's studio. Jock had won his friendship when 'Colonel Lawrence of Arabia' had first been discovered to have enlisted in the R.A.F. A press photographer got into the camp, and Jock, knowing Shaw's feelings, got hold of the camera and smashed it up.

It was of no avail: Trenchard was a timid man, scared of publicity and that Shaw might be thought to be his secret spy—so he turned him out. A clever man would have used the publicity to stimulate recruiting, which would have turned the tables on Little Imp.

I think that my last meeting with Shaw was when he dropped in for lunch at Hilton Hall. H. E. Bates had come over to meet Dorothy Edwards, the young Welsh author of *Winter Sonata* who was staying with us. As he says in his autobiography, he thought her story, *A Country House*, one of the best in our language. Dorothy was a passionate member of the extremist Labour Party, who expected the Revolution to sweep away all forms of injustice within a few years—if not months. Shaw, in his uniform was a hireling upholding the oppressors, though being in the ranks, he was obviously of proletarian origin himself. During lunch, Dorothy, who had read Classics at a Welsh university, said something to me about Greek literature. Shaw joined in, either agreeing or disagreeing with her—it doesn't matter which. Dorothy snubbed him, disagreed with him and assumed superior airs. Shaw was polite—I think he rather liked her—Dorothy downright rude; and I was glad when we rose from table. After Shaw had roared away on Boanerges, his Brough Superior motor-bicycle, I asked Dorothy what she thought of our visitor.

'I thought he was a very ordinary little man, except that he would talk about subjects which he could know nothing about.'

I had taken for granted that she would have known the identity of Aircraftsman Shaw, but she thought he was an acquaintance I had made while learning to fly. She was annoyed when I told her that our visitor had translated the *Odyssey*. My dear Dorothy, longing to wave a red flag over the barricades in Whitehall, had given us one of the worst examples of class intolerance that I can remember. She who was such a sensitive writer was not observant of the world. I once took her up for a joy-ride in my aeroplane. She was eager to record her feelings during the flight. The result was a piece of introspection which might just as well have been written in the Underground railway.

Manning must have the last word.

There is no doubt that of all the interests that Shaw had in his rather unusual life, his last six years in the Air Force represented a haven, represented an object of great devotion, gave him a technical challenge which he couldn't have believed would arise. It came by chance. He took the opportunities made available to him at Mount Batten, and made the best out of them, and with distinction. Purely by chance, arising out of the rescue operations associated with a flying boat crash in Plymouth Sound in 1929, his long association with motor boats began. Once involved, entirely unprofessionally at first, he soon became deeply committed to a personal crusade of technical improvement of R.A.F. safety launches. In retrospect we know that his contributions to the development of new boats of revolutionary design was immense. My own view is that he was one of the prime architects of our Air Sea Rescue Service. Although he did not live to see this service grow beyond its adolescence, I feel sure that had he lived to see the 64-foot launches in operation during the last war, and had known of the thousands of lives they helped to save, he would have felt both contentment and pride in his achievements; something that 'the Lawrence' appeared not to experience after his Arabian venture.

H. E. Bates

H. E. Bates

After reading the manuscript of a novel called *The Two Sisters*, Edward wrote a letter to Miss Bates to say that he had recommended it to Jonathan Cape for publication, and would like to discuss the book with its author. He was surprised to learn that it was the work of a young man.

Bates has described being taken to lunch at the Étoile in Charlotte Street by Jonathan Cape and Wren Howard, and his feelings of astonishment and awe when Edward appeared, leaning on his stick, swathed in scarves and carrying a basket full of his weekly purchases made in the market and delicatessen shops in Brewer Street. To the eyes of youth, he looked a clumsy dancing bear. A mistake, for though age made some movements clumsy, Edward could juggle three eggs at once.

My wife, Ray, and I had recently bought Hilton Hall, between Huntingdon and Cambridge. It was then a cold, sparsely furnished house. Built about 1610, it has great dignity and charm, though it has only eight rooms and additions. Bates lived not far off, at Rushden in the valley of the Nene, so Edward suggested that I should invite him over to stay a night. Bates (who, like H. G. Wells, concealed the name of Herbert under his initials) accepted and proved to be a slightly-built young man with fair hair, blue eyes and a rosebud complexion. Suitably dressed, he could have impersonated a pretty and talented Miss Bates anywhere. Actually he was a keen soccer player and cricketer.

I was planting some lime trees on the boundary of the orchard, and Bates came and held the tree upright like a lance, while I shovelled earth round the roots and then stamped it down all round, before shovelling some more and stamping that down.

Shyness disappears when men are working together, and there could have been no better introduction. Ray was attracted by him and he liked her. Bates's visit had been a success, though our house was cold and bare, and Bates's unwarmed bedroom must have been icy. The friendship, thus begun, prospered.

H. E. BATES

GREAT FRIENDS

In the spring we drove over, along lanes scented with hawthorn, through beautiful (then), forgotten villages—Toseland—Stoughton—Swineshead—Yeldon. After meeting Bates, we climbed a sugarloaf eminence—the Castle Mound, to have our picnic. At our feet, beside a stream, was a tiny inn, once kept by Bates's grandparents. Many of his delightful *Uncle Silas* stories were to spring from his boyhood memories of it and them. Bates was proud of his family: he came of a long line of shoemakers and boasted that one of his uncles still possessed the lasts on which the high boots for Marlborough's cavalry had been made. Shoemakers in the Midlands have always been independent-minded. They had persistently returned Bradlaugh, an atheist who would not take an oath on the Bible, to Parliament, until at last the law was changed so that he could affirm and take his seat. In earlier times their independence had given rise to the proverb, 'the shoemaker should stick to his last', coined by supporters of the Establishment.

After a spell in the boot factory, Bates had explained to his father that he had to be a writer, and his father had agreed to support him for a year while he wrote his first book. If he failed, he would go back to the factory. *The Two Sisters* was the result of his father's faith. He was writing short stories, and Edward, acting as unpaid literary agent, placed them wherever he had influence. Bates soon went down to The Cearne, and Constance and he took to each other. With Edward, Bates talked about writers and writing. With Constance the talk was as knowledgeable—but about flowers. For this remarkable young man was not only a keen soccer player but he had found time to read very widely and to become an expert horticulturist.

Edward discovered to his delight that Bates had read a lot of Turgenev, Tchehov's stories, Conrad . . . in fact the authors which he would have made him read, if he had not done so of his own initiative. He had his own opinions and stuck to them, though he looked like a bud on one of the rose-bushes he was pruning for Constance. She fell rather in love with him, Edward worried about his career and how he could keep his head above water and find time to write.

With his encouragement Bates left Rushden and came to London. A job was needed, and Edward persuaded John Wilson, the canny manager of Bumpus's bookshop in Oxford Street, to take Bates on as an assistant.

John was an old friend of Edward's, but he was a business-man, and after a little while he told him that Bates was not earning his salary and that he would never make a shopman. But he agreed to keep him on if

Edward paid Bates's wages, which he did until enough came in from the stories for him to give up the job. I believe Bates never knew of this transaction, of which Wilson told me after Edward's death.

Even if Bates spent much of his working hours reading the stock instead of doing up brown-paper parcels, I think Bumpus did not have a bad bargain.

Bates had been writing some very good stories when one evening I found Edward greatly perturbed. Bates had written a story, taken lock, stock and barrel from one of Tolstoy's. And when Edward had given him a lecture, Bates had defended himself and had not appeared to realise that his action was criminal. Edward proceeded to a more severe lecture telling him that he would be ruined if such a plagiarism were detected. Some writers are extraordinarily receptive, but Bates was not a slavish imitator, and this lapse was the only one of its kind. I never read the offending story and can only judge it by its effect upon Edward, and by an acknowledgement of the affair Bates made to me many years later.

Bates spent a year over a second novel of 150,000 words long which Edward described as 'Hardy and water', 'unreal'; it was 'facile, flowing, over-expressive, long-winded, romantic and cynical', 'half-baked and there was no question of publishing it'.

However, in spite of this, Edward did not give up faith in Bates's talent. Soon afterwards he was praising two short stories: 'I don't see anything to criticise in either.'

In 1931 Bates married a girl with whom he was in love at Rushden and greatly daring bought an old granary at Little Chart in Kent. Madge was the perfect wife for him. She is strong, enjoys life and was ready to embark confidently on the adventures which lay before them both.

Bates is a master of the short story, and the novella, as he called the longer ones. He has a sharp, clear vision of character showing itself in a situation, and can completely convince the reader. His novels are inferior. This, I think, is because he had not the power of sustaining a narrative. There is a wide gap between the revelation of a character in a situation and the architectural construction of a novel.

After Edward's death in 1937, I worked as one of Jonathan Cape's readers and inherited Bates. He was already an established writer of short stories—but at that time novels sold better, and perhaps this was the reason that he wrote *Spella Ho*. I had a long hard fight over it. I knew, perhaps even better than Edward would have done, what was wrong, for I had become entangled in writing a long novel which would not come right and which I finally abandoned. So I told Bates that large parts of *Spella Ho* must be rewritten. A week or two later, the manuscript returned, rewritten, but with the same faults. And though the book was eventually published by Cape in 1938, the faults remain.

In late August 1939, when war appeared inevitable, I was invited to join the staff of the Director of Intelligence at the Air Ministry and was commissioned as a Flight-Lieutenant. My first duty was to concoct, with Hector Bolitho, a weekly news-sheet to entertain the enlisted men of the R.A.F. Our styles were different. Hector would write about how our Sovereign George VI had taken his wings as a pilot, the rank he held and the medals he was entitled to wear. All very loyal—but which called forth a comment from our Security Officer, Colonel Chambers, 'The aircrews don't want stuff written by a housemaid in Buck House.' I had read in a newspaper that owing to shortage of petrol there were plans to collect and bottle methane gas from sewage farms. I put in this item with the comment: 'During the war, private cars will go by shits and farts.' To my indignation this was cut out as too coarse a joke for our aircrafts-men, so I reproduce it here.

Plans were afoot to employ other writers, who would publicise the R.A.F. instead of trying to entertain its personnel. At that moment I received a letter from Bates asking me if there was any sort of job in the R.A.F. which he was qualified to do. He was obviously the man who would write impressions of the different branches of the air service better than anyone. Although I was suspected of trying to find a cushy job for an old friend, I got Bates into the R.A.F. with the help of Nerney, the Librarian of the R.A.F. who saw that Bates might be the writer they wanted. Getting Bates that job was the most valuable service I did while I was in the Air Ministry.

The stories that he wrote as 'Flying Officer X', *The Greatest People in the World* and *How Sleep the Brave,* were the first result. They were followed by a novel, *Fair Stood the Wind for France.* They were best-sellers on a huge scale. Later Bates was sent out to Burma, an experience which led to his writing *The Purple Plain* and *The Jacaranda Tree.* These novels were best-sellers on the large scale. I thought them fakes, but I rejoiced that Bates and Madge and their sons would be rich people, able to live as they liked and to travel whenever they wished. But I concluded that Bates as a real writer was finished, just as Galsworthy had been. Success is fatal. To my astonishment, Bates went back to writing short stories—as good or better than those he had written in his youth. It seemed miraculous. Indeed it was miraculous. Success on that scale is like selling one's soul to the Devil—but to get the best of both worlds—to touch pitch and not be defiled: that is the rarest thing in literature.

Bates was a very prolific author: he lists 24 novels, 20 volumes of short stories, nine volumes of essays and one of drama, one volume of criticism, two of autobiography, two for children and two as 'Flying Officer X': altogether 61 volumes omitting collections of already published work—all written between 1925 and 1971.

Bates used his relative wealth to transform The Granary on the green at Little Chart into a lovely place with a most beautiful garden full of flowers and with an excellent vegetable one at the side.

He had an eye for pictures and picked up some charming ones at Christie's and Sotheby's from under the noses of the dealers. He liked the Impressionists and had several very good paintings by some of the little known men.

He was a gourmet, and one was given good food and good wine in his house, and in London was invited to lunch at the Caprice restaurant.

He and Madge were fond of travel and particularly of Switzerland. The frail, but muscular, rosebud young man grew stout. There was physically a likeness to H. G. Wells, but the blue eyes were milder. He was an altogether quieter man who was content to enjoy life and not to worry too much about it. Moreover his gifts were very different. He had not had the scientific training which enabled H. G. Wells to foresee the changes which were upon us, he was not a propagandist ready to make hasty judgements. Instead he accepted the world as he saw it, he understood women better than any man writing through the middle half of this century. But both men had the same robust sense of humour. *Mr Polly* and *The Darling Buds of May* belong to the same world. They are amusing but not important.

Bates was as uneven as he was prolific—but artists are judged by their best work, and his short stories rank with those of any writer of our time.

T. H. White

T. H. White

Terence Hanbury White, who was always called Tim, wrote to me: 'I want to make a play out of Sir Walter Raleigh . . . will you tell me what *one* book I am to read . . . as far as the history is concerned? . . . The fellow's character I understand already: it is my own.'

The project came to nothing, so we are deprived of a revealing self-portrait. Though he was never my idea of Raleigh, Tim had the exciting charm one thinks of as Elizabethan.

At one time he believed that Raleigh had written Shakespeare's plays. He may have thought it would not have been out of character to have done so himself, for he had a high opinion of his own talents: 'I know more Irish and European history than anyone else except (if except) Dr Hyde.'

I had got to know him by writing a very laudatory review of *They Winter Abroad*, a lighthearted novel in the style of Norman Douglas's *South Wind*, published under the pseudonym of James Aston. I was then Literary Editor of the *New Statesman*, and Tim a schoolmaster at Stowe. Later I wrote another enthusiastic review of his *England Have My Bones*, and soon afterwards Tim sent me a thirty-pound salmon which he had grassed (the right word) on the River Orchy.

I was an aspirant fisherman, Tim an aspirant author. He had acquired the false impression that I was omniscient, I that he was a master of every field sport. We met seldom but wrote to each other frequently— and a selection of our letters has been published—*The White/Garnett Letters* (Cape, 1968). Tim wrote good letters because he enjoyed life, and could also see himself as a comic figure in retrospect.

On getting to know him I wrote:

First the size of the man, then the brilliant, very blue, rather bloodshot, unhappy eyes, and the patient voice which usually sounded as though he were very carefully explaining something to a child and which would then split with the sudden realisation of an absurdity, or a shared joke. Tim was usually

T. H. WHITE

intensely serious when he made a remark; the comic became apparent as he gave it a second look.

At the end of August 1939 I took my wife and our two boys to stay with him in Mayo, where he had rented a moor on which there were a few grouse at which he could fly his falcons. I had to return to England on the outbreak of war, and it was not until after my departure that they brought down a brace of birds, which Ray made into a pie.

One day we went down to fish for sea-trout in the Owenmore River. But before we had even put our rods up, we realised that fishing was impossible because of the clouds of midges which covered us.

When we were leaving, we passed an old Irish peasant, and Tim called out that fishing was impossible because of the midges. The old man stood trembling with terror at the two large Englishmen in the huge car and plainly understood nothing.

'The midges,' shouted Tim and pointed at his beard which was full of them. 'To be sure, your honour, it is a very fine beard indeed.' Delighted by this unexpected tribute, Tim let in the clutch, and we drove back to Sheskin Lodge.

In September 1939 I joined the R.A.F.V.R. as a Flight-Lieutenant in Air Ministry Intelligence. Tim bombarded me with suggestions for winning the war.

'Do you remember how I nearly invented a revolving Lewis gun? I have had several inspirations of the same or better sort. I can't write them down in a letter but . . .'

He was writing from Ireland, and letters were opened. He did however risk sending me a detailed plan with illustrations which he asked me to communicate to the Chiefs of Air Staff. He proposed that we should maintain a permanent fighter screen over the Baltic Sea by having: (1) A number of oil tankers in the North Sea from which Sunderland flying-boats would be refuelled; (2) These should refuel our Spitfires and Hurricanes while in the air. He did not discuss how the fighter planes were to be rearmed and maintained, or the pilots fed, or rested. Perhaps sandwiches might have been dropped by parachute. Another letter he sent me was to be forwarded to the Admiralty. It contained directions for laying smokescreens.

Tim was in Eire, because in February 1939, I had invited him to come salmon fishing on the little river Dee in Meath. As there were no fish (they had been netted by the locals the day before our arrival) we went to the Boyne, where there was free fishing. Within a quarter of an hour I had grassed a fourteen-pound salmon. My luck so impressed Tim that he decided to stay there after my wife and I had returned to England. She found him lodgings in a neighbouring farmhouse, and Tim remained there, on and off, until the end of the war.

At first he frequently threatened to take an active part in it unless his talents were intelligently employed.

Can you get me anything to do which is not utterly frivolous? In the Air Ministry or for propaganda or anywhere? If you can't, I shall go to Belfast and volunteer as a gunner on merchant ships. My attitude is that I refuse to be a half-and-half: for instance, to take a commission in the army or something like that. If people will not use razors as razors then I think the razor has a right to refuse to be a lawn-mower. It has a right to insist on being a steam-roller. Either I must have a serious occupation as a razor, or I will be quite insane as a garden-roller-able-seaman-cum-lewis-gun. I am 36, I took a First at Cambridge, I once could speak Italian rather fluently and fly an aeroplane very badly indeed. . . I have broadcast and been serialised by the B.B.C., have a contract with W. Disney, and am in this year's Who's Who . . . Failing rational work, as I say, I shall just suit my inclinations and go on convoys.

Tim's inclinations did not lead him to do any such thing.

In another letter he announced: 'I will take any job of any sort you consider ought to be taken: anything to get back to England.'

In another he asked me how he could qualify to fly aeroplanes across the Atlantic as a ferry pilot. He had obtained a pilot's licence because he was terrified of flying and believed that intense fear has a therapeutic effect. After getting the licence he never flew again.

But why all this boasting of being a razor and threats to behave as the majority of Englishmen of his age were doing?

He let the cat out of the bag when he wrote: 'I have come to dread the damage which might be done to my book by people like Godfrey Winn or Beverley Nichols, if they chose to hint a slander at my personal courage.'

However, he ran that risk and soon persuaded himself that he was Irish. His father had been born in Ireland. The same argument could be used to prove that Tim was a Hindu, as he had been born in India. Soon he was addressing me as 'You Anglo-Normans', being himself an Irish-speaking Celt.

Had he not happened to be in Ireland when the war started, he would probably have enlisted and made an excellent Captain, being an inspiration to his men. In any higher rank he would probably have caused trouble.

As to his assumption that his mind was like a razor, nothing could have been more untrue. It was far more like a sheet of blotting-paper, taking an impression of his surroundings. He absorbed any new thing very rapidly, and almost at once believed that he had mastered the subject. It is difficult to know how seriously Tim took his pretensions.

When I first met him I believed him to be a master of, and an authority on, all field sports, which I feel pretty sure he believed himself to be. These were then hunting, fishing, shooting, wild-fowling and falconry. He had tamed many wild animals and kept them as pets: badgers, hedgehogs, grass snakes and barn owls. He claimed to break in horses and he trained gundogs.

He knew Italian, some Irish and translated medieval Latin. Later on he drew in pastels and painted in oils, sailed boats, and went down in a diver's suit. He claimed to be a good carpenter.

He shared certain qualities that I have described in my portrait of Ford Madox Hueffer. Both were dedicated writers who left a large quantity of work, very uneven in merit. The greater part of Tim's was in the form of unpublished journals, illustrated by himself.

Both men found it easy to believe what was to their immediate advantage. Thus, when seeking to marry Violet Hunt, Ford persuaded himself that he had taken on his father's original German nationality. In 1940, during the war with Germany, Tim claimed that he was an Irishman, because his father had been born in Ireland. Ford became a practising Roman Catholic for as long as it seemed possible that it would help him to get his marriage with Elsie annulled. Tim almost became a Roman Catholic, but drew back at the last moment. Both suffered from a touch of megalomania.

Yet two men could not have appeared more different. Tim was physically active, a tireless sportsman in his earlier days. Ford was lethargic. Tim was a stronger character and could never, under any circumstances, have appeared to be 'a jellyfish at bay'.

Both had money troubles and got into debt—but while Ford's were due to poverty and he died penniless, Tim's more serious troubles were due to wealth, which bewildered him and led indirectly to his death.

The most unfortunate example of Tim's power of believing what was to his advantage was the publication of *The Elephant and the Kangaroo*, a farcical description of a second Deluge, this time in Ireland. It contained intimate portraits of the MacDonaghs with whom he had been living for five years. Mrs MacDonagh had mothered him and loved him like a son. She was, moreover, an ardent Roman Catholic. The description of her as a comic character, and of her husband as an idle

clown, could not but cause very great pain and the feeling that she had
been betrayed.

When I pointed this out and told Tim that there were many passages
for which he could be sued for libel, Tim cheerfully replied: 'About
libel, I shan't let it be published or sold in Ireland. Will this do?'

He did not stop to ask whether it was possible to stop it reaching
Ireland, and that when a book is published anyone can read it, or that a
kind friend of the MacDonaghs would be sure to see that a copy fell into
their hands. Nor did he go back and ask forgiveness. The Irish phase of
his life was over: he was going on to pastures new.

During the war I had bought a hill farm in Northumberland on the
banks of the North Tyne. Brownie, Tim's Irish setter bitch, had died in
1944. This was the greatest tragedy in Tim's life. He wrote almost
insane letters with an accusation that Brownie had been poisoned. She
had probably died of old age. But her death took place while he was away
on a drinking bout in Dublin, and though he sought to accuse others, he
believed that his was the guilt, and that she would not have died if he had
been with her.

I told him to buy a puppy and that bringing it up would help put his
grief into perspective. I added, most unwisely, that I would like a
gundog myself, for there were grouse on my new hill farm. I suggested
that he buy a pointer puppy for me and that he should bring up the two
puppies together. The idea that he was helping me led him to take my
advice, and I became the nominal owner of an animal which grew to the
size of a calf.

At the end of September 1945 Tim arrived at Hilton Hall driving his
big S.S. Jaguar car with the two dogs. He was almost penniless, and had
gladly accepted the loan of my cottage in Swaledale for the coming
winter though it would be bitterly cold, and he was likely to be snowed
up in it. The pointer which had been registered as Prince, I renamed
Quince. He kept knocking crockery off the table with his tail.

Brownie's successor, Killie was a most lovely creature: a beech-leaf
red Irish setter bitch. I liked her—no one could help doing so, but I
disliked Tim's treatment of the animal. She ate off his plate at meals.
Although meat was rationed, he would ask for another slice for Killie.
She slept in his bed, she lay on the sofa, one's hospitality was judged by
how well Killie fared. The presence of my pedigree British Blue cats was
a mark against me.

I admire and respect cats and rather despise dogs for their slavish
devotion to man, and to tell the truth I am rather afraid of them. I dislike

their smell and their barking. Dogs know this and dislike me, whereas a handsome tom cat will pick me out from a roomful of people to jump into my lap or perch upon my shoulder.

On two occasions when Tim and I quarrelled he put it down to my liking cats. He hated them.

My wife drove us in to Peterborough, where we could catch the Flying Scotsman as far as Newcastle. Tim showed his mettle when the train drew up. He stopped the guard, practically buttonholed that great man and told him that we had to travel in his van, as the dogs could not be left alone. They were valuable animals.

He looked the ideal sportsman. He was wearing a jacket with a worn leather patch on the right shoulder, a less worn one on the left, breeches, shooting boots and his 'twa-snooted bonnet'. His earnest bloodshot blue eyes and formidable beard gained him a hearing—and, if there had been any doubt, Killie's beauty turned the scale.

Tim and I scrambled in with the dogs, I followed, the guard blew his whistle and off we went, ushered into a bare empty inner sanctum. The only drawback was that there was no seat, and that when I sat on the dirty floor, the dogs licked my face.

Ridley Stokoe farm has two hundred acres of moorland and crag, the home of grouse, black game, hares and rabbits, with an occasional snipe and woodcock. There are pheasants and a covey of partridges in the fields by the river.

Our visit was a disaster. The dogs were untrained and pointed at bumblebees, frogs and even sheep. Then they were disobedient, ran in and chased all the birds off the moor for the rest of the day.

Tim was in a rage owing to his failure to control the dogs and visited it on me: I had led him to suppose that I owned a grouse moor and not a backyard. So we quarrelled. I skip the details, but I formed the opinion that Tim was not a particularly good shot and a very poor trainer of gundogs.

Tim flung himself into every new pursuit with enthusiasm and learned the theory of each with great rapidity. He then believed and made me believe he was a master of the subject. He could write so well and teach what he had just learned convincingly. It was a surprise to find he failed when it came to doing it himself.

From Northumberland we went to Swaledale, where Tim and the dogs settled into my cottage on Whitaside for the winter. Life there is difficult in bad weather, but Tim stuck it out well. He was very poor, but had money enough to buy for £41 the Bestiary which he translated, and to have crates of his books sent over from Ireland. Many of them perished in an outhouse after he left. The difficulties of life were mitigated by the kindness of the dalesmen, and by his charming the landlady of the Punchbowl Inn. He fetched his car from the garage, but did not come in the two miles to see me at Hilton. It was not much use in Swaledale, and he ran up a bill at Reeth for its repair.

I sent him vegetables and—at his request—a hamper full of unrationed delicacies from Fortnum and Mason.

Quince—which I had asked him to dispose of—got Killie with pup. He went down to shop at Low Row on Mondays and Thursdays and had lunch there in the Punchbowl.

In the early months of 1946, he became aware that *Mistress Masham's Repose* had been chosen as Book of the Month in the United States. This was to bring him £15,000. I advised him to go to Mexico. That was impossible, because it would involve exiling Killie, who would not be allowed to return without being held in quarantine for several months. I then told him to go to the Channel Islands. He had to get out of England to avoid having to pay out a large part of his windfall in tax.

In April he wrote to say that he had got engaged to the young girl who was the child heroine of *Mistress Masham's Repose*. In the early summer he brought her to Hilton to stay a night on the way to Duke Mary's, the Swaledale cottage. She took an instant dislike to Hilton Hall, which was soon extended to its occupants. Duke Mary's cottage proved too much for her, and she broke off the engagement, which was fortunate for both of them. Sylvia Townsend Warner wrote in her biography that Tim 'wanted to get married, but had no inclination for it'.

Tim detested all Governments and all their works and especially all forms of taxation. I liked his, possibly prophetic, references to 'the Farewell State' but found repeated references to 'Urinal' (instead of Aneurin) Bevan tiresome. He enjoyed finding variations on the name Milton Waldman—who was then employed by Collins, and who had raised difficulties when Tim said that he would rewrite his books in proof. He abused publishers until he met Wren Howard, and Michael Howard became one of his closest friends to whom he left the many volumes of his daily journal. He thought of publishers as they were regarded at the beginning of the eighteenth century. That is, they were a band of illiterate rogues who lived by swindling authors who starved to death in the attics of Grub Street.

But how much of all this was the result of his love of superlatives? That verbal exaggeration was as much part of him as his sweeping gestures—as his enthusiasms. He loved life and enhanced it. He was never dull.

What were his talents as a writer? His magnum opus, *The Once and Future King*, is full of rambling, nonsensical and conventional moralising about Lancelot and Guenevere, Arthur and Mordred and wicked women. But one can skip through that happily for the sake of the comic passages and the beautiful ones. Merlin, another idealisation of himself, is a rather vulgar figure.

But the knockabout farce: the knights tilting, but unable to do more than catch a glimpse of the opponent once their visors are down, is not only superb comedy but realistic.

The young Arthur's education: flying softly through the night with the owl; recoiling just in time from the pike's jaws; that is masterly, as good as anything in *The Jungle Book*, but more poetical than Kipling. Transcending these lovely passages are Tim's sudden unexpected powers of sympathy and understanding.

Here is a passage from the book I like the best: *The Godstone and the Blackymor*, though it starts with nonsense about me. It is about a Nigerian quack doctor whom he met in a remote village in County Mayo:

He was not welcome in hotels. They would not give him sheets, believing his colour to be dirty. I suddenly saw him in his bare, enemy, empty bedroom, much cleaner than I was—surgically clean—pressing his one suit under the mattress, a lone wolf. . . He kept himself fit and neat and tried 'to take it'. He had to. Like a white man in the depths of the jungle, depending upon his fitness, he was a jungle man in the depths of civilization, a leopard stepping catlike, dainty, though the traffic of Oxford Circus.

Tim's invention is usually schoolboyish and often vulgar: all his best work derives from observation, from a personal *rapport*. Then a sensitive awareness springs into existence.

As in his writing so in his life. In September 1956 he wrote to me:

Some time last winter I began to think about people who were stone deaf and stone blind . . . So I found out the address of an association which tries to help such people and wrote offering to maintain four d/bs on a week's holiday each, paying their fares and expenses, and those of their guides, for of course they can't travel alone. The first one . . . is an enchanting little sparrow of a distressed gentlewoman . . . twice as intelligent as an ordinary woman, as she has to be—as brave as a lioness, five feet high. . . Well, the whole week was a roaring success. I had learned to speak on my fingers before she came. . . She was avid for experience . . . She had never been in a boat, or seen a live fish. We hauled her into a fishing boat in a storm, and she caught four herself! We taught her to swim on her back!. . . She climbed to the very top of the lighthouse, went to a cocktail party, had tea at Government House, and all the time people brought her things to feel and smell . . . She went d/b at the age of about 12— and is now in her fifties . . . She . . . gave me quite as much pleasure as I gave her, and we prattled on our fingers day and night, like two babies in a bath tub.

Puck—for that is the name I knew her by—went to Alderney for her holiday for five years. I had a short correspondence with her. She was indeed remarkable.

So far I have written of Tim's failings. But his doing something, when he thought of the deprivation of the deaf blind, and his imagination in what he did, were typical and explain why so many people loved him and why he won devoted friends wherever he went.

Tim had bought himself a pretty little Georgian house in the main square of Alderney's only town. My first visit was not a success. I was violently sick during the crossing, and the boat could not enter the harbour for several hours owing to the high seas.

Tim was drinking brandy all day and dispensing it to all comers. A self-styled genius complained bitterly that Tim was not maintaining him in the way he expected. The fellow wrote me a catalogue of his grievances after my return to Hilton Hall, and I enjoyed writing him a letter telling him that though it was impossible for *him to* feel gratitude to Tim, it would be diplomatic to pretend to do so when talking to other people, as it would raise him in their estimation. I don't suppose he followed this excellent advice!

Eventually Tim could stand him no longer, stuck a notice, 'BUGGER OFF', on his front door and went out and got drunk.

The parasite wrote to me, 'I took the hint'.

Though I was glad to visit Tim on Alderney, I realised that, however beautiful, it would be intolerable to live on that small island. I was struck by the fact that though Alderney is within a few miles of Cherbourg, Tim had not set foot in France. It would have meant leaving Killie alone for several hours.

Tim had won the Book of the Month prize twice; he now came into a fortune. His Arthurian cycle had been published as *The Once and Future King*. This was now chosen as the subject of a musical to succeed *My Fair Lady*, which had been manufactured from Shaw's play *Pygmalion*. Tim told me he was getting the same royalty as Shaw.

Tim's health had suffered: he was liable to interrupted circulation of one leg, and he was drinking brandy steadily—his doctor having forbidden whisky. Tim's fortune bewildered him. He built a temple in his garden to the Emperor Hadrian—who had succeeded Sir Walter Raleigh as the figure with whom he identified himself. In front of it he put in the worst designed swimming-pool I have ever swum in, and he bought the pinnace of Lady Docker's yacht. That lady, much publicised, was reputed to have a gold-plated Daimler, and a husband who could deny her nothing. He was the Chairman of the Birmingham Small Arms Company until the crash, after which his wife's yacht had to be sold.

When visiting London, Tim came to see me at the Reform Club. He was arrayed in splendour. There were, I think, jewelled cufflinks in his shirt of the thickest silk. His suit was new from Savile Row, his shoes hand-made. And over all he wore a long cloak lined with scarlet silk, and in his hand he carried a gold-knobbed malacca cane.

It was not Sir Walter Raleigh, nor the Emperor Hadrian, who stood before me. It was Sir John Falstaff. Yes, he was *Falstaff in funds*. He was, as he said, 'solvent'. But otherwise he had no idea of the extent of his fortune.

He had come over to London to adopt the son of a distant relative. He would play Merlin to a young Arthur. But the boy had the good sense to refuse to be adopted.

Tim had been lucky in a way far more important than riches. He had bought a cottage next door to his house, and this was occupied by Lieutenant-Commander Harry Griffiths and his wife. Griffiths became Tim's gardener and factotum. It was impossible to restrain Tim, but Harry Griffiths looked after him, went sailing with him, and so on.

My second visit to Alderney was delightful. Julie Andrews, who was Guenevere in *Camelot*, and her husband, Tony Walton, were staying close by in a small cottage. They had become very fond of Tim, and he of them. I helped Julie to grill lamb chops, and in the evening after some of us had drunk a lot of champagne, she consented to sing for us. Everyone was happy.

I had written a rather tough letter to Tim some years before after he had said that the heroine of my novel *Aspects of Love* ought to have her 'crenellated, lace, Victorian pants' taken down and been beaten. In my reply I wrote: 'Your remarks about taking down a woman's drawers and beating her smack of flagellation—a perversion which, as you know, is frequent among those who have been much caned as small boys, among schoolmasters and judges who have been able to inflict corporal punishment with impunity.'

Tim had brooded long over my letter. He had given my book to Tony Walton to read, with our letters, and wrote to tell me that Tony agreed with me.

Now Tim led me into a room where we should not be interrupted, and told me that he was a sadist, and explained what unhappiness it had caused him. When a sadist falls in love with a normal person he must either be false, or tell the truth—and whichever he does he repels and loses his beloved. Intimacy—sexual intimacy—is impossible. Tim went on to say that he believed he had inherited the tendency from an ancestor of his father's who was a notorious flagellant. This seemed unlikely. Tim was maltreated by his mother and flogged at school.

If only this confidence had been made twenty years earlier, I should have been a kinder and more understanding friend. As it was, it came too late. Our friendship—with my usefulness—was drawing to a close. But there was an extraordinary proof that our relationship was not merely the superficial one of two men at cross purposes. One evening at Hilton Hall the telephone rang. It was Tim telling me that he had just recovered consciousness after an operation. He was in St Thomas's Hospital, and he begged me to come and visit him. At the end, his voice wavered, became blurred, and there was silence.

I went up to London next day and presented myself during the visiting hours. Tim gave a cry of astonishment:

'How on earth did you know that I was here? It must be telepathy!' He had completely forgotten that when he came to from the anaesthetic his first thought had been to ring me up, and that he had done so before losing consciousness again.

It was Tony Walton's father, a doctor, who forced Tim to have his leg treated and finally the operation. It was not entirely successful, and the trouble recurred. Tim's body had not stood the strains that he so recklessly imposed on it, and he developed a coronary and had not long to live. This was a warning that Dr Walton gave his young daughter, Carol, who had courageously agreed to go with Tim as his secretary and manager on a lecture tour of the United States.

He had been drinking, with intervals, heavily for years. But he realised that he would put Carol in an impossible position if he drank heavily on the lecture tour. Because he would not hurt her, he had the remarkable will-power to cut out drinking altogether on the tour. His lectures were, on the whole, a success, because his audience responded to his personality.

When the tour was over she flew back to England, and Tim embarked on a cruise designed to take him to Greece and Egypt. He drank very heavily during the voyage, and when the ship docked at the Piraeus he was found dead in his cabin.

Harry Griffiths flew out and buried him within sight of Hadrian's arch, and had this inscription cut upon his tombstone:

T. H. WHITE
1905 – 1964
AUTHOR
WHO FROM A TROUBLED HEART
DELIGHTED OTHERS
LOVING AND PRAISING
THIS LIFE

The fault in my friendship was that I had never sufficiently realised, or made allowances for, the troubled heart.

Carson McCullers

Carson McCullers

For, I think, a few months only, a young officer, Captain Emmanuel, was attached to the military wing of the Political Warfare Executive, where I was working. It was the worst moment of the war—a week or so after the Dieppe raid, when a large number of Canadian soldiers had been sacrificed in order to prove that it was impossible to land troops on a well-defended beach. I was not afraid that Britain would be invaded, or conquered, but neither did I believe that the German army would ever be defeated. That meant that for the future all the careless forms of happiness, and all the worthwhile forms of artistic activity were at an end. Creative literature and painting—the free arts, would be forgotten, and I myself should never write the kind of books I valued.

Then suddenly Captain Emmanuel, with whom I don't think I had had even the most formal dealings, came up to me and asked:

'Have you ever read this book by a young American woman? I think you would like it.'

I opened *Reflections in a Golden Eye*, read it at a sitting, and rose up a different man. I was ready to shout with triumph.

War might burn out the freedom of imagination and culture and all the creative arts of Europe, but what I had been mourning was alive and immortal. Here was a girl in America who was writing the kind of story that I most admired. I could laugh at regimentation, at the God of War and that lunatic Hitler, who had brought death to millions. Art and Literature were still living in my lifetime.

The mood of pessimism that I had been in may seem mad to young people today, but it was shared by thousands at the time of which I write.

I may have written to Carson then, or I may have waited and expressed my admiration in a review of her next book. And she, I am certain, wrote back, so that she was aware of my existence.

Some years later I had been giving a few lectures in the United States

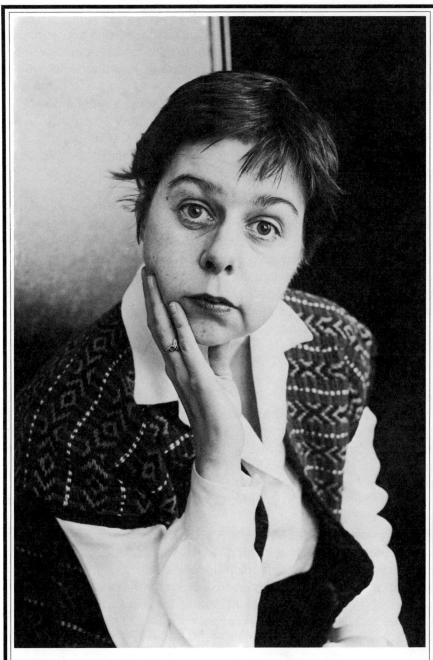

CARSON McCULLERS
photograph by Cecil Beaton

and was in New York. One day Shusheila Lall told me that her husband, Arthur, who was the Indian Ambassador to the United Nations, wished to give a party in my honour, and asked whom I would most like to be invited to meet me?

'Carson McCullers,' I replied. By that time, though I was unaware of it, she was very ill—one side paralysed with rheumatoid arthritis. As a result she was in continual pain. She drank to alleviate it—not because she was an alcoholic. And what follows is an account which I wrote almost immediately after our meeting.

I went up in a lift to the Ambassadorial apartments. There was a strong smell of Indian cookery. Then I was ushered into a large saloon where the Ambassador receives his guests. There was Shusheila, more beautiful than ever, in the white silk sari and a little white silk jacket embroidered with golden stars, which I had asked her to wear. And beside her, sitting on the sofa, a crumpled figure with short rat-eaten orange hair, wearing a Japanese green and peacock blue kimono, with a black rubber-ferruled stick beside her. It was Carson McCullers.

My heart beat with emotion and alarm. I bent over her, sat down beside her and she kissed me three times. Her eyes were dark and full of pain. Her complexion was that of some overcooked grey vegetable tinged with poison. Doesn't soda sometimes discolour food so that it becomes unpalatable?

Her lips trembled, and she spoke in a very low voice. I told her that I thought she was the best writer America had produced since Henry James—no exaggeration. I told her how in the darkest days I had been given *Reflections in a Golden Eye*, and that she had made me believe we might live to see again a world in which art was a ruling force in our lives. I told her as much as I could, and then guests poured in, and I had to be introduced.

It was a world of diplomats: a youngish Russian and his wife (no doubt in the secret police) turned up, then another Slavonic couple, then a torrent of stray people. And of course Arthur Lall. He is small, even for a Bengali, strikingly good-looking with an air of gay self-possession. Perhaps his power of taking his own importance light-heartedly had helped him in his career.

He led me up to a huge man, who spoke, unexpectedly, in the voice of a self-conscious pansy. And pansy he was, suffering from a feeling of persecution because his boy-friend had not been asked. He had come himself, because he didn't know whether the omission had been unintentional—on the part of Indians. I escaped and went back to

Carson, who was drinking her second tumbler of Scotch on the rocks.

We began talking, and as I was asking whether she was coming back to Europe I saw a cockroach run across her lap and dive into the folds of her kimono. No doubt the kitchen was alive with them. The white-coated servants were in a state of excitement: they trembled like sporting dogs that had scented game, they were trembling as they handed glasses or refilled them—they had brought Carson some food and a cockroach.

We were given plates of fried chicken, curried pimentos and meat balls. Carson could only pick at her chicken with one hand, so I took her knife and fork and cut it up. She abandoned Scotch for a tiny glass of claret. Mine was refilled many times.

Krishna Menon, then Ambassador at Washington, had rung up—in despair at not having been invited. Shusheila repaired the oversight, and soon the great man arrived and stumped about the room with a walking-stick. He was the great man, very consciously the great man of the party, obsessed by his own greatness. A clever, vain, intellectual face, but harried by something—just as the actor's face is harried by knowing that however great he may be, he is not really Hamlet, Prince of Denmark, or Macbeth, the King of Scots. He was introduced to me and Carson. Monroe Wheeler said: 'Our greatest author, who has a play running on Broadway.'

'It closed tonight,' said Carson, in tones of death.

At that moment the cockroach ran out of the folds of her kimono towards the empty plate. I made a pass at it, but the intelligent insect reversed and darted back into safety.

'We have met before,' said Krishna Menon. 'We met often in the office of the *New Statesman*.' He talked of Kingsley Martin. I asked him if he felt that he were the same man as he was in those days. It was odd meeting ambassadors, when all the Indians I had known were revolutionaries.

'Bepin Chandra Pal, for instance.'

'He was a leader who had never arrived anywhere,' said Menon.

'He sat on the fence. He had been in prison and did not want to go back there,' I explained.

Krishna Menon's face became gloomy. I had, without knowing it, hit on a painful topic. For Krishna Menon had never been in prison. It was the one blot on an otherwise brilliant career.

He was rising. 'I must read one of your books,' he said to Carson graciously.

'You should see her play, now running on Broadway!' said Monroe Wheeler.

'It came off tonight,' said Carson.

My host, Arthur Lall, wanted to tell me that Krishna Menon had so much enjoyed meeting me. A woman in yellow assailed me.

'Mr Gar*nett*. You understand *me* and I know that I understand *you*. Your work has made me what I *am*. I am entirely your responsibility.' She surged towards me. In another moment we might have coalesced. I took a step back, she came forward. Monroe Wheeler had given me a cigar, and when she had got me against a wall, I protected myself with the lighted tip. I was pinned against a chair in which an Indian woman in a pale green sari sat airing her beauty silently, like a slender daffodil.

'Don't try and get away from me, Mr Gar*nett*,' cried my pursuer.

'My host is signalling to me.' I broke away, abandoning my glass of champagne—a small price to pay, and consoled myself with Carson's, as she had gone back to Scotch.

Suddenly Shusheila appeared carrying a two-stone Alsatian puppy, while the huge bitch mother barked and leaped furiously.

'Carson wanted to see them,' said Shusheila.

The bitch sprang with claws ripping silk saris. Human cries mingled with the canine uproar.

Carson nodded like a seasick traveller looking at the waves breaking over the ship. Her lips trembled, but the words would not come. I held her hand, and she squeezed my fingers tight.

'In two years' time, when you come back, you must come and stay with me,' she said.

'Or you'll come over to live in France.'

'I haven't the money.'

'You'll write. Take care of yourself, so that you really can write.'

Her face lit up with a smile of happiness. I looked at my watch. Half-past eleven. 'I have got to be going now.'

'In a year or two years, whichever way it is, we'll be together,' she said. Carson leant over and we kissed. The Russian and Polish *chargés d'affaires* with their wives (members of the secret police), Arthur Lall, Shusheila, the languid daffodil, and Monroe Wheeler, stood watching as we kissed again and again.

'Take care of yourself.'

'Yes, I'm going to write stories.'

I took leave of Arthur and Shusheila. A Slav diplomat bowed.

'*Do svidanya*,' I cried gaily in Russian.

'I am Polish,' he said. An expression of nausea had crossed his hitherto bored features. I escaped into the night.

I was in New York again two years later. On the eighth of December it was very cold, but everything was revealed in a sharp light, and the bare woods were beautiful as the bus took me to the last stop before Nyack. Following directions, I got to Carson's house in time for lunch. The Negress, who I think had known her from a child, brought us our food, carried away the dishes and summed me up in a careful look from her dark eyes.

Carson said: 'Isn't it wonderful—I am going to stay with you next summer, or perhaps in the spring.' Then she told me that she had a great friend, whose husband, a famous surgeon, was taking his sabbatical in the coming year, and that they were going to take her along with them.

I was overjoyed, and at once began making plans for putting a bed in my study downstairs, so that Carson should not have to climb our staircase, the treads of which are bevelled by three hundred years of use.

I was a little disappointed to hear that a friend was coming directly after lunch to take us to visit her father who lived in the woods nearby. He had started as a painter after the First World War and had then become the most famous potter in America.

'Some survival of Thoreau, or William Morris,' I said to myself with annoyance. I had been brought up amongst such characters. I had had all I wanted of them, and Carson would sit silent while I was being told that handicrafts were the cure for all social ills.

I had misjudged Henry Poore. After being demobilised in 1919 he had, to save his sanity, rejected the present American way of life and had gone back to its earlier pattern. He owned some rocky forest land at Haverstraw, near the Hudson River, and decided to build a house on it. He began by cutting the oak trees he would need later, so as to let them season. Then he had turned quarryman and had hewn out the stone he would need for the walls of his house. Then, becoming a mason, he had shaped them, and only then had he started building. His house was on a hillside. At first it was one room with stone walls. After he had sawn the oak trees into beams, he needed help so that while he dropped the beams into the slots in the walls, his neighbour held the rope of the pulley from which they swung. Henry was a real man. He was not only a lumberer, mason, carpenter and builder, but a true artist. I asked him why he had given up painting to become a potter.

'Painting takes too much out of me. After an hour or two I am exhausted. But I can spend all day happily moulding clay with my hands and not become tired.'

He had married and so had built more rooms onto his house. One walked down steps to the kitchen, and there was a storey above. Early on he had decided to make only a few pots and to sell them for very high prices, otherwise he would have enslaved himself competing with established potteries. As a result his work is to be found only in the houses of the very rich and in museums. I liked all the work I saw, but did not much care for the large ceramic fountains he had made for the gardens of millionaires. But I was only able to judge them from photographs. Before I left he gave me a book he had written, *The Hands of the Potter*. It was true that Carson had sat silent, or speaking to Henry's daughter Anne, in whispers, but the visit had been worthwhile and had reassured me that she had neighbours who loved her and admired her and who would come to help, if her black servant could not cope with an emergency.

After we got back, Dr Mary Mercer came in. She was a tall, fair, intelligent woman. It was with her and her husband that Carson had told me she was going to Europe on his sabbatical.

Suddenly it seemed to me that I had been talking to Frankie Addams, that Carson was the heroine of her own masterpiece, *The Member of the Wedding*, the adolescent girl who convinces herself that her brother will take her with him and his bride upon their honeymoon. What I had read and had heard spoken on the stage, was being rehearsed, in a slightly different form, by its author. I was torn with pity. Carson needed love so much.

Dr Mercer left. I turned the conversation away from the visit to Europe and Carson told me about Tennessee Williams, about writing plays and about the book she was going to write, or had partly written. She had been drinking Scotch on the rocks all day, and by bedtime I had drunk far more whisky than usual. However I was not too drunk to help Carson up to her bedroom and to kiss her goodnight before I rolled into my bed to sleep like a log.

Next morning I had to rise early to catch the morning bus to New York. It had snowed a little when we left Henry Poore's, and it had snowed a little more during the night. The snow was not deep, but the air was icy: one of the coldest mornings I can remember. I waited for a long time at the bus stop. Finally I risked the bus coming along and not stopping for me and walked into Nyack. I reached the stop just in time and then warmed up inside the bus, as we drove through fairyland.

232

CARSON McCULLERS

When we approached New York, the snow suddenly got deeper, and when I got out at the bus station, not far from the Washington Bridge, the spectacle was extraordinary.

New York had suffered a blizzard: the streets were empty, buried two feet deep. Men were already shovelling, here and there, on the sidewalks. But what was most surprising were the cars, which were hidden under mounds of snow. Where they had been parked nearly head to tail, the wall of snow was continuous, with only a slight dip where one car below ended and the other began. I walked almost the full length of Manhattan Island through a city where there was scarcely anyone moving. On the big avenues a few people struggled along, but in the cross streets connecting them, there was no life, and the snow was deep.

I was warm with exercise and I rejoiced; I could have shouted with pleasure seeing the helplessness of that great city pitted against the power of nature. It was December the ninth, 1959.

As I had foreseen, Carson was not a 'member of the Mercers' sabbatical' but nevertheless she did come to Europe, and our next meeting was in London.

Osbert Sitwell could have made millions as a publicity agent if he had had articles to promote more essential to the ordinary housewife than his sister Edith, his younger brother Sacheverell and himself. As it was he worked miracles. On Edith's seventieth birthday in October 1957, the *Sunday Times* gave a lunch and published a symposium in her honour. And on her seventy-fifth birthday, 9 October 1962, a celebration concert was organised in her honour in the Royal Festival Hall. Carson McCullers attended, and although she is said to have accepted a lecture engagement, she told me that her fares had been paid to Europe and back, a suite in the top of Claridge's provided, as well as a nurse companion to look after her, all by a Sunday newspaper, as Edith had asked for her to be present.

In her book about Edith Sitwell's old age, *The Last Years of a Rebel*, Miss Salter describes Carson visiting Edith's house at Greenhill, wearing a fur coat and carpet slippers and managing to walk down a corridor with a stick and supported by a nurse. Miss Salter was surprised to see her looking so young—a 'perennial adolescent' in spite of having the whole of her left side paralysed and a face that 'could contain a smile for a few seconds only'.

During this visit to England I saw her twice in her suite in Claridge's. She was ill and in pain, but she was as happy as a small child in the early hours of Christmas morning. She was thrilled by all that was being given her. She declared that she had never stayed in such grandeur, and she even seemed a little afraid that the management would find out that she didn't belong in such surroundings. The unfortunate thing was that she was being flown back to America almost at once, and that in any case she was too ill, as I realised, to come and stay at Hilton Hall. At the end of my visit she asked me to come back next day to lunch.

She was thrilled by the food being carried up on trays by flunkeys, though she regretted she had not been able to bring her much-loved Negress. She had not been able to come, as she had her own family to look after, and the air fare would have been double.

Carson must have known she was doomed to an early death. But she was entirely without self-pity. She was as happy as a child because of what was being done for her. Her sister Margarita Smith tells how Carson loved being given presents. It was because she was a child who needed to be loved so much. Presents were a proof that the people who gave them loved her. I wished that I had known this, or I would not have gone to Nyack empty-handed.

Two years later, at the end of October 1964, I paid my second visit to Nyack. It was the Indian summer, and the colours of oak and sumach and dogwood were lovely in the sunshine.

Carson was feeling ill, crouched forward gripping her tumbler of Scotch, the best pain-killer.

She began telling me about the book she was writing, would write, or had written. I must have misunderstood, if as I thought later, she was speaking of *Clock Without Hands*. I had not read it, and when I did, I believed she had achieved the impossible of writing that masterpiece when she was sick to death and could hardly hold a pen. Only later did I notice that the American edition was published in 1961—three years before our conversation. But she may have been speaking of another book or have even been confused herself.

I did not stay long on that visit and went not long after lunch, for I saw that she ought to rest. Also it had become unbearable listening to this great writer telling me about a masterpiece which could never be written. Actually she went on writing until the final haemorrhage of which she died.

Two years later I paid my last visit to Nyack, on 12 November 1966, less than a year before Carson's death.

She was ill and exhausted, but eager to talk and glad to see me. For the first time she told me a little about her life and her marriages—for she

234

was married twice, each time to the same man. He was James Reeves McCullers, and I think she was very much in love with him. And then Carson, sipping her big tumbler of Scotch, told me how the second marriage became impossible because he drank so much, and they had no money.

Carson told her sister that she became each of the characters that she was writing about; that when she wrote about Captain Pemberton in *Reflections in a Golden Eye* she became a male homosexual, and so on. That is part of the reason why she is a great writer. And another is that she wrote from her imagination. She didn't like the word *prose* because it sounded *prosaic*. Prose should have some of the qualities of poetry, and poetry should have the clarity and meaning and sense of good prose.

She insisted that she could only write well about the South, and that the same was true of Faulkner, but that Hemingway was the most cosmopolitan of modern Americans.

But it is not the locale that matters, but depth of understanding. Because of this, Carson is more like one of the great Russians than any American of this century. Her first novel, partly written before her first marriage when she was nineteen, and published when she was twenty-three, *The Heart is a Lonely Hunter*, has for its hero a man to whom self-seeking men come for guidance, a deaf mute, and he has in common with Prince Myshkin, the hero of Dostoevsky's *The Idiot*, that love which we feel is goodness.

Acknowledgements

I have to thank Professor J. T. Boulton and Cambridge University Press, the editor and publisher of the new edition of D. H. Lawrence's Letters for permission to publish D. H. and Frieda Lawrence's letters to me, for which acknowledgement is also made to Laurence Pollinger Ltd and the Estate of the late Mrs Frieda Lawrence Ravagli. I also thank my wife, Angelica Garnett, for permission to quote her reminiscences of her aunt, Virginia Woolf; and Professor Quentin Bell and my wife for her letters.

My thanks to Air Commodore Manning are of a different order of magnitude. My portrait of Aircraftsman Shaw owes its value almost entirely to him. For he provides first-hand evidence of the last years of Lawrence 'of Arabia', when he was Aircraftsman Shaw of the R.A.F. Marine Craft Section, which has hitherto not been available.

Some of this book has appeared in a somewhat different form in the following writings of mine:

The Golden Echo (1954)
The Flowers of the Forest (1955)
The Familiar Faces (1962)
Introduction to W. H. Hudson, *The Purple Land* (1951)
'Some Writers I Have Known: Galsworthy, Forster, Moore and Wells' in *Texas Quarterly* (Autumn 1961)
'E. M. Forster and John Galsworthy' in *A Review of English Literature* (January 1964)
'Virginia Woolf' in *The American Scholar* (Summer 1965)
'Forster and Bloomsbury' in *Aspects of E. M. Forster* (1969)
'Maynard Keynes as a Biographer' in *Essays on John Maynard Keynes* (1975)

Index

INDEX

INDEX

INDEX